Refugees in Canada

Thomas Ricento

Refugees in Canada

On the Loss of Social and Cultural Capital

palgrave
macmillan

Thomas Ricento
Werklund School of Education
University of Calgary
Calgary, AB, Canada

ISBN 978-3-030-76452-4 ISBN 978-3-030-76453-1 (eBook)
https://doi.org/10.1007/978-3-030-76453-1

This Palgrave Macmillan imprint is published by the registered company Springer Nature Switzerland AG.
The registered company address is: Gewerbestrasse 11, 6330 Cham, Switzerland

Despite all of the dangers that we might face back in Colombia, I think that it is better to take that risk given all of the frustrations we have experienced here. At least we would have the opportunity to have our careers and a decent life in our country … The way we are living here we feel as if we have lost our dignity while we have to beg for help in order to survive.

—Fernando, Colombian refugee, December 9, 2010

You are like in an open prison. You see others living, but you are not living. As soon as you are living that situation, it finally makes you sick.

—Patrick, Congolese refugee, October 7, 2010

There is a Somali saying which goes like this: "when there are no choices, you are in shackles" I mean you have to work with what you have and focus on your own interests, so I have to say that, indeed, our housing was not satisfactory. We were not satisfied with the housing conditions but that is what life has offered and dictated.

—Aziza, Somali refugee, October 23, 2010

For refugees everywhere
and for those who work on their behalf

Preface

How can we understand what is meant by a nation? We would agree that a nation is fundamentally an aspiration enunciated by discourses that coalesce over time around particular themes connected to beliefs about the social good, the social order, and societal values. A nation-state presupposes a legal or some other 'official' claim to legitimacy by some authority/authorities to a geographical area inhabited principally by people who have some attachment to those particular themes (although varying proportions of the nation-state will not share such attachments and will, to varying degrees, view such legal and territorial claims as illegitimate and even unlawful), and who proclaim a shared cultural identity based on history, religion, race/ethnicity, and/or language. History is the accounting of the nature and unfolding effects and consequences of those claimed foundational identities over time, usually told from the perspective of the 'founders' (or, alternatively), the 'victors' in the struggles that led to the construction of the nation-state; as Henry Kissinger (1964) famously put it: "History is the memory of states." We know that in most modern nation-states, including Canada, many classes of people were excluded from full membership in the nation-state before, during, and after its founding. For example, in Canada, women gained the franchise in 1918 (although women in Quebec did not receive full suffrage until 1940), 51 years after Canadian Confederation (1867); in the United States, women had to wait until 1920 to gain the vote, 144 years after the Declaration of Independence (1776) declared that "all men are created equal." Enslaved Africans arrived on the American continent in 1619 (157 years prior to the Declaration of Independence) and were granted suffrage in 1870 with passage of the 15th Amendment (94 years after the Declaration of Independence), but were effectively denied the vote by the imposition of multiple barriers in various states, including literacy tests and poll taxes, and by other devious means designed to restrict access to the ballot that were not fully overturned until passage of the Voting Rights Act of 1965 (189 years after the Declaration of Independence, and 346 years after the arrival of enslaved Africans; however, voter suppression of African Americans still exists in parts of the United States today). Amerindians, who arrived in North America at least 12,000 years ago, continue to suffer the effects of European colonization. While the successful struggles to obtain universal suffrage along with other advances in civil rights among excluded categories of persons in liberal democratic states can be celebrated, the undeniable fact is that democratic nation-states, such as Canada, still deal with challenges to ensure the full integration of groups that have experienced various degrees of marginalization because of their perceived or ascribed race/ethnicity/national origin/gender, among other reasons. An important challenge resulting from the nonstop movement of people across the globe, usually from less wealthy to more wealthy countries, concerns long-held ideologies[1] about the nature of national identity, about who merits consideration for full inclusion as a bona fide member of the nation-state, about the role government should play in integrating newcomers, and, as importantly, about the role society should and can play in the integration process.

This book takes a hard look at social, political, and economic challenges facing Canada today from the perspective of the experiences of refugees and other classes of immigrant newcomers. Although these challenges are not new, they are worsening, based on available government data and the findings of scholars who have investigated these topics over the past decades. The stated goal of federal government policy has been to provide support to ensure the successful integration of all classes of immigrants into Canadian society. The Immigration and Protection Act (1991) states that a key goal of the legislation is "to promote the successful integration of permanent residents into Canada, while recognizing that integration involves mutual obligations for new immigrants and Canadian society." A key question raised by the research reported in this book is 'to what extent is Canadian society fulfilling *its* obligation to promote the successful integration of all classes of immigrants?' For example, is Canadian society more porous, more accepting of racial, cultural, religious, and linguistic diversity today than it was when Prime Minister Mackenzie King, in 1947, gave a speech in parliament in which he announced that the policy of the government was to increase the national population by encouraging immigration, while also warning that "the people of Canada do not wish, as a result of mass immigration, to make a fundamental alteration in the character of our population" (Haque 2012: 32)? Five years later, in 1952, the government announced annual quotas on Indian (15), Pakistani (100), and Ceylonese (50) immigrants that remained in place until 1962 (Haque 2012: 33). Changes in immigration policies in 1962 removed the quotas from 'undesirable' countries, but even in the 1960s Canada was being characterized as a binational country that was comprised of two 'founding races' (White Anglophones and Francophones), essentially ignoring the just claims of Indigenous peoples as the 'original founding race,' while lumping all 'other' inhabitants into the 'multicultural' category, an undifferentiated group of immigrants and their descendants whose languages and cultures were (at best) of secondary importance compared to those of Anglophones and Francophones.

Given the wide range of personal characteristics recent immigrants possess, it is dangerous to make any generalizations as to the likelihood they will (or won't) eventually be 'successfully integrated' into Canadian society, assuming that integration is their goal in moving to Canada (which it may not be). Yet, aggregate data described in great detail in this book provide compelling evidence that recent immigrants (this includes refugees) are less likely to be employed in the professions they practiced in their country of origin, that their rates of unemployment will be higher, and that their earnings will be lower (controlling for education) than comparable Canadian cohorts, among other important differences. Many explanations are offered to account for these facts, including lack of 'Canadian work experience,' non-native language skills in English or French, and lack of 'appropriate' sociocultural sensitivities (i.e., not being able to 'behave' the way Canadians are expected to behave), among other explanations.[2] While these explanations may have merit in some cases, they are not adequate to account for the overall outcomes experienced by the most well-educated and professionally credentialed immigrants over the past 25 years.

In order to properly interpret these attested facts in the Canadian context, I have examined both quantitative data (such as rates of (un)employment, underemployment, earnings, wealth disparities, and gender biases) that have been cross-tabulated with immigrant class, national origin, race/ethnicity, length of time in Canada, educational attainment, and language competencies, and contextualized these data through the personal experiences of six refugee families living in Calgary, Canada, that involved in-depth interviews with family members over a nine-month period.

Canadian society, historically and in the present day, has operated within an assimilationist ideological framework in which monolingualism (predominately 'standard' English) and monoculturalism (predominately the values and beliefs associated with a White/European/Christian settler society) constitute the baseline norms which 'non-Canadians' should adapt to if they expect to become 'Canadians' (whether or not such adaptation means they will truly be accepted as 'Canadians' by the dominant majority in the 'host' country).[3] The research reviewed in this book demonstrates the effects of these ideologies on 'others' whose ethnicities, ascribed racial categories, languages, and 'nonstandard' language varieties have placed them in the margins of society and at a disadvantage in a labor market that devalues their 'foreign' education, credentials, and work experience, even though such marginalization runs afoul of the 'official' tropes that claim anti-racism and equality of opportunity and treatment to be foundational and essential Canadian values. If interculturalism and multiculturalism are to be more than one-way streets in which 'others' are expected to conform and assimilate to 'Canadian' societal norms (impossible for visible minorities) while 'society' does little or nothing to accommodate, respect, support, and learn from the diversity of cultures and languages that enrich and expand the sociocultural compass, then the social and economic challenges facing immigrants in Canada described in this book have little chance of being overcome, despite official efforts, through the tweaking of policies, to improve the situation.

Calgary, AB, Canada Thomas Ricento

Notes

1. Ideology, as used throughout this book, generally means "having to do with legitimating the power of a dominant social group or class" (Eagleton 1991: 5). Woolard and Schieffelin (1994) provide a useful review of the various ways in which the terms 'ideology' and 'language' have been used in anthropology, sociolinguistics, and cultural studies.
2. The lack of recognition of foreign-earned academic and professional credentials is an undeniable barrier to labor force integration, especially for those immigrants from non-Anglophone and developing countries.

3. A definition of culture was provided in the *Report of the Royal Commission on Bilingualism and Biculturalism* (Volume 4 (1969: 11)): "Culture is a way of being, thinking, and feeling. It is a driving force animating a significant group of individuals united by a common tongue, and sharing the same customs, habits, and experiences. It is a style of living made up of many elements that colour thought, feeling and creativity, like the light that illuminates the design of a stained glass window ... This definition is applied essentially to the two dominant cultures of Canada, those of the francophone and anglophone societies; to a certain degree it also fits the other cultures in this country."

References

Eagleton, T. (1991). *Ideology: An introduction*. London: Verso.

Haque, E. (2012). *Multiculturalism within a bilingual framework: Language, race, and belonging in Canada*. Toronto: University of Toronto Press.

Kissinger, H. (1964). *A world restored*. New York: Grosset and Dunlap.

Royal Commission on Bilingualism and Biculturalism. (1969). *Report of the royal commission on bilingualism and biculturalism*. Volume 4: *The cultural contribution of the other ethnic groups*. Ottawa: Queen's Printer.

Woolard, K. and Schieffelin, B. (1994). Language ideology. *Annual Review of Anthropology*. 23: 55–82.

Acknowledgments

Research is always a collaborative effort, and the project that forms the core of this book is no exception to that general rule. I especially want to recognize Dr. Andreea Cervatiuc and Dr. Vladimir Pavlov for their important contributions as team leaders and researchers; they contributed to all aspects of the project, including development of questionnaires and interview protocols, organizing schedules for interviews with the immigrant families, and coordinating with the ten interpreters/translators who worked throughout the project, as well as entering, organizing, and analyzing interview transcripts, among many other duties. The quality and extent of their collaboration cannot be overstated. I also want to thank the ten interpreters who worked with our team; their contributions included translating all consent and information forms from English into one of seven different languages, providing interpretation for all participants in Phase I and Phase II of the project, and later translating recorded interviews into English; we could not have achieved the high level of trust and acceptance by our refugee collaborators without the kindness and patience exhibited by the translators, all of whom originally arrived in Canada as refugees themselves. We appreciate the cooperation and support given to us by the Resettlement and Integration Services Coordinator at the Calgary Resettlement Centre (a pseudonym); she welcomed us with open arms and shared her insights based on years of experience working with the refugee community in Calgary; she also introduced us to prospective translators and other personnel at the Centre who helped us better understand the processes and goals of refugee resettlement in Calgary. I also want to recognize contributions made by Dr. Fabiana MacMillan and Dr. Sepideh Massoudi who collaborated with me and Dr. Cervatiuc on an earlier research project in one of the largest Language Instruction for Newcomers in Canada (LINC) ESL programs in Calgary; our findings from that project provided ideas and research tools that informed the project that will be discussed in this book.

I owe a special debt of gratitude to the Werklund School of Education, University of Calgary, where I was Professor and Research Chair in English as an Additional Language from 2007 to 2018; funds from that Chair enabled me to assemble teams of graduate students, postdoctoral fellows, and recent PhDs to conduct the sort of in-depth and time-consuming longitudinal research required to understand the range of challenges faced by refugees in their integration into Canadian society. Without that support, this research (and this book) would not have been possible.

I would also like to thank an anonymous reviewer of the book proposal who provided critical and important feedback, including ideas on how the book could be improved; a number of those suggestions have been taken up and incorporated in the final product.

Finally, I offer my sincerest thanks and admiration for the refugee families that participated in the research project conducted in Calgary from 2009 to 2011; this book is dedicated to them. My goal throughout the project was to share their personal stories in their own words in order to provide greater texture and detail on some of their lived experiences they shared with us during the nine months that we conducted interviews in their homes in Calgary. I believe their stories will help readers of this book better understand the complexity of their journeys; while all of the refugees we interviewed were grateful to have escaped often terrible, life-threatening experiences in their countries of origin, most were also intimidated by the unexpected demands of adapting to a new society in which their languages, professional credentials, and life experiences were often not recognized as legitimate or relevant for entering the Canadian workforce. Their stories are similar to those of our own ancestors who arrived in earlier generations; it is important to have our memories refreshed periodically lest we forget the paths that brought everyone to Canada over the past several centuries, except for First Nations peoples whose presence on the North American continent predates the arrival of

European settlers by at least 12,000 years. Humility, empathy, and gratitude should be our guiding principles in how we evaluate 'others' in our communities; although it is a commonplace, we need to be reminded that our humanity fundamentally unites all of us in our common pursuit of a better life—and better world—for ourselves, our families, and future generations.

Contents

CHAPTER 1

The Problem

Abstract There is a mismatch between Canadian federal government immigration policies which are geared to attract high-skilled workers with high levels of education and fluency in one of the two official languages and the actual experiences of immigrants in Canada, who, controlling for education and language, experience unemployment and underemployment at significantly higher levels than native-born Canadians. Despite Canada's preference for highly skilled immigrants, and despite the fact that immigrant professionals bring significant human capital resources to the Canadian labor force, a number of studies have shown that many highly educated immigrant professionals experience deskilling and devaluation of their prior learning and work experience after immigrating to Canada.

Keywords Immigration policies • Foreign credential recognition • Citizenship • Refugees • Family class refugees • International Medical Graduate • Canadian work experience

Introduction

There is a mismatch between Canadian federal government immigration policies which are geared to attract high-skilled workers with high levels of education and fluency in one of the two official languages and the actual experiences of immigrants[1] in Canada, who, controlling for education and

T. Ricento, *Refugees in Canada*,
https://doi.org/10.1007/978-3-030-76453-1_1

language proficiency in an official language (English and/or French), tend to experience unemployment, underemployment, and lower earnings at significantly higher levels than native-born Canadians with similar qualifications. This gap has only increased in the twenty-first century, and it is likely to get worse.

According to Ikura (2007), several factors have contributed to negative outcomes for new arrivals in Canada, including lack of recognition of foreign credentials, lack of Canadian work experience, deficiencies in one or both of the official languages, and inadequate labor market information, among other factors. Subsequent research has confirmed the findings of Ikura while expanding the number of variables measured that allow for even more fine-grained analyses that differentiate outcomes based on factors not previously available to researchers.[2] The case studies that will be discussed in this book deal with the experiences of refugees in Canada (both Government Assisted Refugees (GARS) identified through the United Nations High Commissioner for Refugees (UNHCR)) and Refugee Claimants (often referred to as asylum seekers, individuals who apply for refugee status upon arrival in Canada). However, it is worthwhile to consider whether (and to what degree) the experiences of refugees are different from the experiences of those from other immigrant classes (Economic Class and Family Class),[3] especially with regard to their earnings, employment status, and general integration into the Canadian workforce.

One of the most comprehensive syntheses of research relevant to the principal themes to be discussed in this book is *Foreign Credential Recognition Research Synthesis, 2009–2013* (Kelly 2014). This work was conducted by Centre of Excellence for Research on Immigration and Settlement (CERIS), funded by Citizenship and Immigration Canada. Kelly (2014) deals with five main areas of Canadian immigration: settlement and integration, foreign credential recognition, citizenship, multiculturalism, and refugees. The synthesis of research covers the period 2009–2013 and lists more than 400 sources. The research discussed is subsumed under the following headings: Labour Market Integration: Assessing Outcomes and Trends; The Determinants of Outcomes; and The Costs of Incomplete Foreign Credential Recognition. In what follows, I summarize key findings related to internationally trained immigrants[4] and their experiences in Canada that are discussed in Kelly (2014).

Reitz, Curtis, and Elrick (2014) note that the proportion of immigrants with a university degree increased from 20.8% of those who arrived in 1994 to 45.6% in 2001 and remained at that level through 2009, and that the proportion of immigrants with university degrees in 2006 was nearly three times as high as for the native-born population for men (44.2% vs. 15.0%), and nearly two and one-half times as high for women (38.7% vs. 15.2%). However, nearly half (47%) of immigrants with postsecondary education had a Canadian degree, reflecting (in part) the cohort of childhood immigrants who arrived with their parents and progressed through the Canadian educational system. Yet, despite this clear advantage for immigrants in terms of educational capital compared to the native-born Canadian population, Plante (2010), using 2006 census data that examined earnings of immigrants who earned their qualifications outside Canada, found that full-time workers in the 25–64 age group had median earnings of $40,800 compared to $49,000 for immigrants educated in Canada, and $49,300 for Canadian-born workers with a postsecondary education. Lo et al. (2010) found that immigrants who obtained their highest education in the United States, the United Kingdom, Australia, New Zealand, and South Africa, controlling for many other variables (age, gender, visible minority status, period of immigration, fluency in an official language, working in a regulated occupation or not, and metropolitan area of residence) earned as much or more compared to those with Canadian education working in the same occupation and city; credentials obtained from non-English-speaking countries had a negative effect on wages, with the greatest negative effect for degrees and diplomas from East Asia, closely followed by West Asia/Middle East/Africa and South Asia. The smallest negative effects on wages are degrees/diplomas from the Caribbean, Central and South America, and Continental Europe (Kelly 2014, p. 21). The role played by country of education also varies by credential held; for example, Plante (2010) found that "while more than 90% of immigrants with credentials in medicine from New Zealand, Sweden, Australia, the United States and the United Kingdom reported working as a physician or in an occupation requiring similar or higher skill levels, this was the case for less than a quarter of those with similar credentials from Japan and South Korea" (Kelly 2014, p. 22). Buzdugan and Shiva (2009) found that education, work experience, and official language proficiency strongly correlate with immigrant incomes, but that Canadian work experience is a stronger predictor of income for immigrants than education, especially in the long term (Kelly 2014, p. 15). Reitz, Curtis, and Elrick (2014) calculated the Canada-wide lost earnings due to both lower returns to education and underutilization of immigrant skills and found that the dollar value of a bachelor's degree for immigrant men, relative to Canadian-born men, declined from 80% in 1996 to 67% in 2006. This means that immigrants are "... paid less than equally qualified native-born Canadians even when they work in occupations at the same skill level" (Kelly 2014, p. 19).

Adamuti-Trache, Anisef, and Sweet (2013) discuss the importance of 'occupational prestige' to de-professionalized immigrants who are often left with less than favorable career options because of barriers to professional accreditation (see, e.g., Blythe et al. 2009; Guo and Shan 2013; Walton-Roberts 2012; Zikic et al. 2010). One consequence of the underutilization of skills and occupational mismatch can be seen on immigrants' health. Chen, Smith, and Mustard (2010) use Longitudinal Survey of Immigrants to Canada (LSIC) data to show that respondents who were overqualified for their job were more likely to report a decline in mental health over a relatively short period of four years (Kelly 2014, p. 34).

Philip Kelly, lead researcher and author of the Final Report (2014, p. 38), reflecting on the more than 400 sources examined in the period 2009–2013, concludes, "[T]here appears to be a persistent devaluation of non-Canadian credentials but upon closer inspection this bias is much greater towards certain source countries, and in some fields of expertise, than others. It is also clear that visible minority status, location of residence, language abilities and length of residence are all variables that matter in this process."

Turning now to labor market outcomes specifically among refugees to Canada, Picot, Zhang, and Hou (2019), using the Longitudinal Immigration Database, examine the labor market outcomes of refugees from 13 source countries with large inflows to Canada over the period 1980–2009. Cohorts from these countries were identified, and their outcomes were tracked for up to 15 years after entering Canada; variations in earnings and employment rates were compared and then the researchers examined whether human capital characteristics, program of entry, or local labor market conditions could explain such variation (Picot et al. 2019, p. 9). The results showed a very large variation in employment rates and average earnings among the 13 identified refugee groups; interestingly, very little of the variation in earnings among refugee groups could be accounted for by differences in observable human capital characteristics, economic conditions, or the program of entry to Canada[5] (Picot et al. 2019, p. 5). In general, educational attainment, language skills (in English or French), economic conditions, and the program under which a refugee enters Canada does not explain why refugees from some countries earn more than those from other countries. The earnings of family-class immigrants were higher than those of refugees during the first full year in Canada (for both men and women); however, after 15 years in Canada, refugees from the former Yugoslavia, Poland, and Colombia had earnings higher than their family-class counterparts entering during the same period. Refugees from countries such as China, Pakistan, Afghanistan, Somalia, Iraq, and Ethiopia earned substantially less than family-class immigrants, even after 15 years in Canada (Picot et al. 2019, p. 24). An interesting finding is that the effect of the program type by which a refugee entered Canada (see endnote i) tends to be greater during the early years in Canada; in the longer run, refugees learned more about job opportunities and experienced language and occupational training which may have reduced any advantage that refugees in one program held over refugees admitted through other programs, initially. Another interesting finding is that human capital, economic, and source country characteristics accounted for very little of the earnings differential very early after immigration, but accounted for a large portion of the differences after five to ten years in Canada (Picot et al. 2019, p. 30). With regard to the effects of the ability to speak English or French upon arrival in Canada, there is a marked difference between different categories of persons landing in Canada either as immigrants or refugees: 38% of the refugees in the sample spoke English or French compared to 61% of family-class and 78% of economic-class immigrants who spoke one of the languages (Picot et al. 2019: 16). This can be explained by the fact that government-sponsored refugees and refugee claimants are granted permanent resident status on humanitarian grounds as persons fleeing extreme dangers to their lives and the lives of family members rather than on the basis of a point system required of non-refugee applicants that awards points (24 out of a total of 100) for the ability to speak one of Canada's official languages. Within all categories of refugees, there were great differences in educational attainment and language spoken at the time they landed in Canada. Quite low levels of education were found for refugees from Vietnam, Cambodia, Laos, Sri Lanka, Ethiopia, El Salvador, Somalia, and China. Fewer than 10% had a university degree, compared to 18% to 26% of refugees from the former Yugoslavia, Poland, Colombia, and Pakistan who had a university degree. While over 70% of refugees from the former Yugoslavia, Poland, Vietnam, Cambodia, Laos, and El Salvador spoke neither English nor French on arrival, refugees arriving from Sri Lanka, Somalia, and Pakistan had very high rates of speaking English (over 75% at landing). Only refugees from Vietnam, Cambodia, and Laos had both low levels of education and a low proportion of English or French speakers, yet these refugees did quite well economically (Picot et al. 2019, p. 14). Taken together, these findings suggest that there is a great deal that is not understood about labor market outcomes among the refugees from the 13 source countries examined in this study. Some groups do well initially, but over time they do less well compared to refugees from other countries; privately sponsored refugees do better than other categories of refugees initially, but that advantage disappears over time as well. The authors (Picot et al. 2019, p. 31) offer a possible explanation to account for the fact that differences in observable human capital characteristics, economic conditions, and the program of entry to Canada explained none or very little of the much lower than average earnings of the refugee groups with the lowest earnings: "One possible explanation is that the education that these groups received in their source countries may have been of lower quality or have been perceived to be of lower quality, thereby affecting the possibility of finding jobs that matched their education level or the wages employers were willing to pay the university-educated in particular." Their hypothesis is supported by a separate regression analysis they conducted that showed that university-educated refugees from Somalia, Afghanistan, Pakistan, and China earned little more (from $1100 to $4400 per year) than their counterparts who graduated from high school; this is in contrast to refugees from Poland, Colombia, and Sri Lanka whose earnings advantage for a university degree was in the $11,000–$12,000 range (Picot et al. 2019, p. 31). The authors note that other unknown factors may be relevant to some of the variation in earnings across source-country groups examined in their study.

While the research project that provides the data to be described and discussed in this book focuses on the lives and experiences of refugees in Calgary, Canada, it is important to look at the broader Canadian landscape with regard to outcomes of refugees and all classes of immigrants over time. It is simply not the case that over time all immigrants, refugees, and their descendants become fully integrated citizens, especially with regard to gaps in earnings, compared to other groups of Canadians. For example, Lightman and Good Gingrich (2012, pp. 125–126) note a general consensus exists that "... the disadvantage that new immigrants face initially and over time is more severe for 'non-Europeans' or 'visible minorities' than for immigrants from 'traditional source countries'" (Banerjee 2009; Frenette and Morissette 2003). Pendakur and Pendakur (1998, 2007) show that "... Canadian-born men and women who are not white face large and significant earnings gaps in comparison to white workers, with certain ethnic groups (such as Caribbean-origin men and women, and Aboriginal men) faring considerably worse than white workers across the full distribution of work characteristics". More recently, examining Canadian-born ethnic groups in Canada over three census years (1996, 2001, and 2006), Pendakur and Pendakur (2011) find that people identified as South Asian and Black, especially in the cities of Montreal and Toronto, fare poorly in comparison to the majority White population. Regression analyses that control for personal and job characteristics show minimal evidence of improving outcomes over time or across generations. Immigrants, and especially those coming from "non-traditional" (i.e., predominantly non-White, non-Western European) source countries, are also found to earn less than Canadian-born and in the past 40 years have seen a consistent and disproportionate decline in their earnings upon entering the workforce (Banerjee and Lee 2015; Green and Worswick 2012). Other research shows that immigrants, despite having higher average levels of education than Canadian-born workers, are almost twice as likely to experience low income (Shields et al. 2011) and suffer negative impacts of a recession first and longer (Picot and Sweetman 2012).

There is no 'quick fix' for the problems identified in the research discussed above with regard to both short-term and long-term outcomes for immigrants, refugees, their children, and future generations. While research on particular cohorts of immigrants and refugees can provide useful guidance to policy makers in areas of immigration and resettlement policy that can be improved, there remain also deeper and longer-term challenges that need to be addressed with regard to earning differentials among various cohorts of immigrants, refugees, and their descendants.

In the following part of this chapter, I consider some of the challenges in the province of Alberta with regard to the situation faced by International Medical Graduates (IMGs); this discussion will provide more specificity to the challenges faced by a particular category of workers in Canada: physicians.

Limitations of the Point System for International Medical Graduates

In 1967, the government of Canada developed a point system in order to increase both the quantity and quality of labor resources in the country. Under the point system, 40% of the possible total of 100 points is allocated to educational attainment and proficiency in an official language (English or French).[6] However, as is stated in the information provided to applicants for permanent residency, there is no guarantee that a person who is granted permanent residence will be able to find employment in the field for which he or she has qualified in their home country. Thus, having a BA or graduate degree, or even a professional degree, while enhancing an applicant's chances of gaining Permanent Residence status, does not mean that the applicant should expect their skills, training, credentials, or experience to be accepted or valued in the Canadian labor market. Furthermore, while a person may be awarded points for having the ability to speak and write English or French, that recognition does not necessarily satisfy the language requirements for many positions in the Canadian workforce. And, as was reported in the previous section, research points to overt and covert discrimination of immigrants from certain regions and countries of the world based on their racial, ethnic, cultural, educational, or linguistic background.

With regard to professionals who land in Canada, whether as government-sponsored refugees, privately sponsored refugees, refugee claimants, or through other classifications, such as family-class or economic-class immigrants, decisions as to their qualifications to work in the professions they practiced in their countries of origin are made by professional societies within each province or territory; because of the large number of organizations with the authority to evaluate and regulate professional credentials (5 provincial assessment agencies and more than 400 regulatory bodies), along with the various types of requirements imposed by employers, internationally trained professionals are often unaware of how and by which body their credentials should be assessed: "The lack of specific information available to prospective and new immigrants on Canada's foreign credentials systems and processes is a barrier to their successful integration into the Canadian labour market" (Ikura 2007, pp. 18–19). Criteria for granting credentials often include standards for language proficiency, as measured by scores on the Canadian Language Benchmark[7] assessment as well by performance on written and oral exams in various professional fields, such as medicine, engineering, and accounting. For example, in Alberta, in order to be qualified to apply for a medical or surgical residency, International Medical Graduate (IMG) applicants have to perform satisfactorily on a multiday exam (the OSCE: Objective Structured Clinical Examination) that requires IMGs to perform in a role play, with actors playing patients, to assess their communicative skills (in English) interacting with patients. In addition, they must pass two written exams on their professional scientific and medical knowledge, as well as achieve an overall score on the TOEFL (Test of English as a Foreign Language) of 95–100 (out of a possible 120 points) and a sub-score in listening of at least 25 (out of a possible 30 points). However, even if an IMG achieves criteria on all of these professional and language requirements, there is no guarantee that he or she will be admitted to a residency, a prerequisite toward eventual licensure to practice medicine in Alberta. In Alberta, the College of Physicians and Surgeons and the Alberta Medical Association (AMA) limit the number of IMGs who will be admitted into Medical or Surgical Residency positions each year in the province of Alberta, which has been about 10% of all positions available in recent years, roughly 10 spots out of 100 available. The basis for admittance to a residency for IMGs is not strictly **criterion-referenced** within the entire pool of qualified applicants, but rather is **norm-referenced** within the pool of qualified IMGs who must compete with **other** IMG applicants for the 10 spots out of 100 that are allocated to IMGs. In other words, there is a quota system for IMGs which greatly reduces the likelihood that a qualified IMG will be admitted to a medical or surgical residency.[8]

Comparison of IMGs in Canada and the United States

Is Canada different from other industrialized countries in how decisions are made with regard to procedures for licensing IMGs to practice medicine? McDonald et al. (2015, p. S116) analyzed the process of immigrant selection and occupational outcomes of international medical graduates in the United States and Canada. They found that in Canada, where a point system has been in place, "IMGs are less likely to be employed as physicians than are IMGs in the United States, where employer nomination is a more important entry path for IMGs." The authors found that of those who studied outside Canada (N = 2721), 57.2% are working as physicians, compared to 91.2% (N = 6471) who studied in Canada. In contrast, in the United States, 87.1% (N = 5091) who studied in the United States are practicing physicians, while 73.5% (N = 1628) who studied outside the United States are practicing physicians (p. S122); thus, IMGs are nearly 2.5 times more likely to be practicing physicians in the United States compared to those in Canada. Wanner (2001, p. 147) claims that nonrecognition of foreign credentials and prior work experience is the "... central immigration issue of the new century not only in Canada, but in all postindustrial societies receiving immigrants." Therefore, while this book will focus on the Canadian context, the findings have implications for the integration of highly skilled professionals in other industrialized countries, especially in countries in which English is the dominant language. While the principal rationale for controlling the qualifications for professional accreditation is to ensure high standards and safeguard the public from harm, such rules and regulations also have the effect of discriminating against persons whose formal training and professional experience may be different from, but not necessarily inferior to, the training and standards imposed by Canadian professional societies. Multiple studies have shown that while immigrants from developing countries have encountered difficulties with their foreign credentials and work experience, those from developed Anglophone countries, for example, the United States, Australia, England, and New Zealand, have relatively successful experiences (Mojab 1999; Reitz 2001; Frenette and Morissette 2003).

Despite Canada's preference for highly skilled immigrants, and despite the fact that immigrant professionals bring significant human capital resources to the Canadian labor force, a number of studies have shown that many highly educated immigrant professionals experience deskilling and devaluation of their prior learning and work experience after immigrating to Canada (Basran and Zong 1998; Krahn et al. 2000; Li 2001; Mojab 1999; Reitz 2001; Banerjee 2009). In applying a one-size-fits-all criterion to measure immigrants' credentials and experience, liberal universalism fails to answer the following questions: Who establishes the criteria? Whose interests are represented and served by these standards? What constitutes valid prior learning? What should we do with knowledge that is valid but different? What forms of knowledge become the Canadian 'equivalent'?

Why the Loss of Cultural Capital Should Concern Canadians

There are many reasons why the loss of cultural capital[9] should be of concern to Canadians. First, the economic future of Canada is highly dependent on the recognition and utilization of the cultural capital immigrants and refugees bring to Canada, especially their professional training, credentials, and experience. According to a recent report from Statistics Canada titled "The Canadian Immigrant Labour Market: Recent Trends from 2006 to 2017" (Yssaad and Fields 2018), the share of immigrants in Canada's population in the year 2036 would stand between 24.5% and 30.0%, compared with 20.7% in 2011; these proportions would be the highest since 1871. Starting in 2031, more than 80% of Canada's population growth will come from immigration, compared to about 67% in 2011. By 2036, nearly 50% of Canada's population will be made up of immigrants and second-generation individuals, that is, non-immigrants with at least one parent born abroad; this share of the population was 38.2% in 2011. Yet, according to data from 2017, gaps in employment and unemployment rates between immigrants and Canadian-born aged 25–54 are significant; immigrants landed five or fewer years had an employment-rate gap compared to the same age group of persons born in Canada of 14.2%; for immigrants landed more than five to ten years earlier, the gap was 6.8%; and for immigrants landed more than ten years earlier, the gap was 2.0%. It should be kept in mind that these statistics are overall averages and mask disproportionally larger gaps for different categories of immigrants who likely experienced far lower employment rates at different points after they landed in Canada compared to native-born Canadians (discussed previously in this chapter). It is clear that the long-term fate of Canada's economic prosperity[10] and social cohesion will be significantly impacted by the experiences of immigrants and their descendants in all aspects of Canadian life. Second, the claim that Canada is a multicultural 'mosaic' that embraces diversity and provides meaningful opportunity for all newcomers to succeed is in danger of becoming an empty slogan that does not reflect reality on the ground; this could lead to cynicism and frustration and civic disengagement, resulting in increased out-migration of immigrants to other countries, as well as reduction in the influx of new immigrants. Third, at a deeper level, the current status of Canada as an officially bilingual nation with a mandate that supports, at least at a superficial level, multiculturalism, but which provides little support for the teaching and learning of heritage and immigrant languages, is at odds with the rapidly changing linguistic landscape throughout the country, especially in the major metropolitan areas of Toronto, Montreal, and Vancouver (Ricento 2013, 2017). For these, and many other reasons, critical analyses of the impediments to the successful integration and meaningful participation of newcomers into Canadian society are needed more than ever, and they need to be taken seriously; this requires that researchers gain a deeper and wider perspective on the actual lived experiences of immigrants that transcends a cursory analysis based on merely looking at official statistics on employment, rates of learning of official languages, and rates at which the children of immigrants attend and graduate university, compared to rates for Canadian-born (their rates are higher). The research presented in this book is a response to this call for a deeper qualitative analysis by sharing the experiences of recent refugees within the context of the broader picture of the statistical data and policy analyses on the experiences of refugees and non-refugee immigrants in Canada over the past 20 years. The goal is to bring to life the actual experiences of refugees, using their own words, to convey the range of experiences, emotions, successes (and failures) they have endured in their first years of living in Canada. I view my role in this endeavor as providing a platform for their voices and stories to be heard, because for the most part, they do not have a voice in the development of policies and practices at the local or national level that will influence—if not determine—the kinds of opportunities and lives they, and their children, will have, today, tomorrow, and in the foreseeable future.

Notes

1. In this book, the term 'immigrant' applies to all categories of persons who arrived in Canada through any of the immigration programs offered by the government of Canada unless a specific program category is identified in the discussion.
2. Some promising new sources of data that have yielded important results include the monthly Labour Force Survey, which has included an immigration question since 2006, and the IMDB, which links immigrant landing records with tax file data (Kelly 2014, p. 2).
3. On average, Canada has offered permanent residency to about 250,000 immigrants and refugees from more than 190 countries each year over the past decade (CIC 2010). Between 2011 and 2016, 60.3% were granted

permanent resident status through the Economic Immigration Program, 26.8% arrived under the Family Class Program, and 11.6% were refugees.

4. In his summary findings in this report, Kelly uses the term 'immigrant' to include all categories of persons who arrived in Canada through all immigration programs, including refugees; however, in one section of the report, he does provide data based specifically on analysis of refugee outcomes.
5. Refugees typically enter Canada one of four ways: (1) government-assisted; (2) private sponsorship, which accounted for one-third of the refugees; (3) the In-Canada Asylum Program (i.e., they were already in Canada when they applied for refugee status), which accounted for one-quarter of the refugees; and (4) as refugee dependents, who accounted for only 3% of the refugees (Picot et al. 2019, p. 28).
6. In 2006, the number of points allocated to educational level was increased from 12 to 25, and the number of points allocated to knowledge of an official language (English or French) was increased from 15 to 24, so that nearly half of the total of 100 points that is used to decide who will be admitted to Canada were allocated to educational level and knowledge of an official language.
7. The Canadian Language Benchmark (CLB) is a task-based language proficiency instrument on a 12-point scale, divided into three levels: stage 1 (Basic Proficiency), stage II (intermediate proficiency), and stage III (advanced proficiency). There is also a French version of the CLB.
8. According to Dr. xxx, Dept. of Family Medicine, University of Calgary, in the province of Alberta the Alberta Medical Association (AMA) sets aside a percentage of places (i.e., a quota) for International Medical Graduates for residencies; the quota is around 10%, so that if there are 100 residencies available in a given year, around 10 are allocated for IMGs; therefore, the system is not merit-based within the total pool of applicants, but rather on a bifurcated system in which IMGs compete with other IMGs within their allocation of 10% of the total applicants.
9. Following Bourdieu (1986), cultural capital includes both embodied forms (e.g., language/language variety) and institutionalized forms (e.g., educational credentials).
10. Reitz, Curtis, and Elrick (2014) use census data to present a calculation of losses due to both lower earnings for immigrants and less access to skilled employment. In constant 2011 dollars, they estimate that these aggregate losses to the Canadian economy rose from $4.80 billion in 1996 to $6.02 billion in 2001, to $11.37 billion in 2006.

References

Adamuti-Trache, M., Anisef, P., and Sweet, R. (2013). Impact of Canadian post-secondary education on occupational prestige of highly educated immigrants. *Canadian Review of Sociology/Revue Canadienne de Sociologie* 50 (2), 178–202.

Banerjee, R. (2009). Income growth of new immigrants in Canada: Evidence from the Survey of Labour and Income Dynamics. *Industrial Relations* 6 (4), 466–488.

Banerjee, R., and Lee, B. Y. (2015). Decreasing the recent immigrant earnings gap: The impact of Canadian credential attainment. *International Migration*, 53(2), 205–218.

Basran, G.S. and Zong, L. (1998). Devaluation of foreign credentials as perceived by visible minority professional immigrants. *Canadian Ethnic Studies* 30, 6–23.

Blythe, J., Baumann, A., Rhéaume, A., and McIntosh, K. (2009). Nurse migration to Canada. *Journal of Transcultural Nursing* 20 (2), 202–10.

Bourdieu, P. (1986). The forms of capital. In J.G. Richardson (ed.), *Handbook of Theory and Research for the Sociology of Education* (pp. 241–58). New York: Greenwood Press.

Buzdugan, R., and Shiva, H. (2009) Labor market experiences of Canadian immigrants with focus on foreign education and experience. *International Migration Review* 43 (2), 366–86.

Chen, C., Smith, P., and Mustard, C. (2010). "The prevalence of over-qualification and its association with health status among occupationally active new immigrants to Canada." *Ethnicity & Health* 15 (6), 601–19.

CIC (Citizenship and Immigration Canada). (2010). *Evaluation of the Federal Skilled Worker Program.* Available at: http://www.cic.gc.ca/english/resources/evaluation/fswp/.

Frenette, M. and Morissette, R. (2003). 'Will they ever converge? Earnings of immigrant and Canadian-born workers over the last two decades', Analytical Studies Branch Research Paper Series, Catalogue no. 11F0019MIE, no. 215 (Ottawa: Statistics Canada 2003).

Green, D. A., & Worswick, C. (2012). Immigrant earnings profiles in the presence of human capital investment: Measuring cohort and macro effects. *Labour Economics*, 19(2), 241–259.

Guo, S. and Shan, H. (2013). Recognition of qualifications and competencies of migrants: Canada. International Organization for Migration (IOM).

Ikura, J. (2007). Foreign credential recognition and human resources and social development in Canada. *Canadian Issues* (Spring), 17–20.

Kelly, P. (with research assistance from Lualhati Marcelino and Catherine Mulas). (2014). *Foreign credential recognition research synthesis 2009–2013.* A CERIS Report submitted to Citizenship and Immigration Canada, Ottawa.

Krahn, H., Derwing, T., Mulder, M., and Wilkinson, L. (2000). Educated and underemployed: Refugee integration into the Canadian Labour Market. *Journal of International Migration and Integration* 1(1), 59–84.

Li, P.S. (2001). The market worth of immigrants' educational credentials. *Canadian Public Policy* 27(1), 23–38.

Lightman, N. and Good Gingrich, L. (2012). The intersecting dynamics of social exclusion: Age, gender, race and immigrant status in Canada's labour market. *Canadian Ethnic Studies*, 44 (3), 121–145.

Lo, L., Damsbaek, N., Phan, M., Kelly, P., Lemoine, M., Fang, T., Preston, V., Tufts, S. (2010). Place of Study of Highest Education: Are Degrees/diplomas from Inside and Outside of Canada Valued Differently in the Labour Market? Toronto Immigrant Employment Data Initiative, TIEDI Analytical Report 14. http://www.yorku.ca/tiedi/doc/AnalyticalReport14.pdf.

McDonald, T., Warman, C., and Worswick, C. (2015). Immigrant selection systems and occupational outcomes of International medical graduates in Canada and the United States. *Canadian Public Policy* 41, Supplement 1, August, S116–S137. Toronto: University of Toronto Press.

Mojab, S. (1999). De-skilling immigrant women. *Canadian Women Studies* 19 (3), 123–128.

Pendakur, K., and Pendakur, R. (1998). The colour of money: Income differentials across ethnic groups. *Canadian Journal of Economics* 31 (3), 518–548.

Pendakur, K., and Pendakur, R. (2007). Minority earnings disparity across the distribution. *Canadian Public Policy* 33 (1), 41–61.

Pendakur, K., & Pendakur, R. (2011). Color by numbers: Minority earnings in Canada 1995–2005. *Journal of International Migration and Integration*, 12 (3), 305–329.

Picot, G., & Sweetman, A. (2012). Making it in Canada: Immigration outcomes and policies. *IRPP Study 29*. Montréal, QC: Institute for Research on Public Policy.

Picot, G., Zhang, Y., and Hou, F. (2019). Labour market outcomes among refugees to Canada. Analytical Studies Branch Research Paper Series 419. Ottawa: Statistics Canada.

Plante, J. (2010). Characteristics and Labour Market Outcomes of Internationally-Educated Immigrants. Print. Culture, Tourism and the Centre for Education Statistics. Ministry of Industry: Statistics Canada. http://www.statcan.gc.ca/pub/81-595-m/81-595-m2010084-eng.pdf

Reitz, J.G. (2001). Immigrant skill utilization in the Canadian labour market: Implications of human capital research. *Journal of International Migration and Integration* 2 (3), 347–378.

Reitz, Jeffrey, Josh Curtis, and Jennifer Elrick. (2014). Immigrant skill utilization: Trends and policy issues. *Journal of International Migration and Integration* 15 (1), 1–26.

Ricento, T. (2013). The consequences of official bilingualism on the status and perception of non-official languages in Canada. *Journal of Multilingual and Multicultural Development*, 34 (5), 475–489.

Ricento, T. (2017). Conceptualizing language: Linguistic theory and language policy, pp. 13–29. In H. Peukert, T. Hagen, and I. Gogolin (Eds.), *Dynamics of Linguistic Diversity*. Amsterdam: John Benjamins.

Shields, J., Kelly, P., Park, S., Prier, N., & Fang, T. (2011). Profiling immigrant poverty in Canada: A 2006 Census statistical portrait. *Canadian Review of Social Policy*, 65/66, 92–111.

Walton-Roberts, M. (2012). Indirect pathways into practice: A comparative examination of Indian and Philippine internationally educated nurses and their entry into Ontario's nursing profession. *CERIS Working Paper Series*. CERIS The Ontario Metropolis Centre. http://www.ceris.metropolis.net/wp-content/uploads/2012/10/Final-Report-Walton_Roberts-CERIS.pdf.

Wanner, R.A. (2001). Diagnosing and preventing "brain waste" in Canada's immigrant population: A synthesis of comments on Reitz. Journal of International Migration and Integration, 2 (3), 417–28.

Yssaad, L. and Fields, A. (2018). The Canadian immigrant labour market: Recent trends from 2006 to 2017. *The Immigrant Labour Force Analysis Series*. Ottawa: Statistics Canada.

Zikic, J., Bonache, J., and Cerdin. J. (2010). "Crossing national boundaries: A typology of qualified immigrants' career orientations." *Journal of Organizational Behaviour* 31 (5), 667–86.

CHAPTER 2

The Researcher and the Researched

Abstract The work and views of Karl Marx, Dell Hymes, and William Labov are discussed in order to illustrate how research in the social sciences can and, in fact, should be scientifically rigorous, creative, and ethical, while being responsive to social conditions and systemic relations that are inimical to human flourishing and societal well-being. Persons conducting research must be aware of and pay attention to how their research can impact the lives of individuals and society, in general, even though the researcher is not in a position to know how his or her findings will be taken up and used by interested parties over time.

Keywords Political economy • De-skilling • Karl Marx • Alienation • Social exclusion • Dell Hymes • William Labov • Ethnography of communication • Non-standard language

It is important to provide background information on the rationale and goals of the research project conducted in Calgary between 2009 and 2011 that this book is largely based on. To do this, I must spend some time explaining my views on epistemology and on the role and responsibilities of the 'researcher,' including the very idea of 'research' itself in the social sciences, before I get into the details of the project itself in Chap. 3.

The questions pertaining to the role of the researcher, his or her 'positionality' in the 'research space,' determining whether the research

T. Ricento, *Refugees in Canada*,
https://doi.org/10.1007/978-3-030-76453-1_2

benefits the 'researched,' and whether or not researchers who uncover causes of social injustice have an obligation to support positive change in the lives of people whose lives and circumstances they have investigated, have been well-covered in various literatures (for a recent and highly relevant discussion with regard to language policy research, see Johnson 2016; Ricento 2015). Rather than reviewing the vast literature on the role(s) and obligations of researchers and the myriad views on the nature of knowledge,[1] which can be abstruse and tendentious, I will highlight the work of Dell Hymes and William Labov, two people whose research advanced not only our understanding of language in society, but also how beliefs about language, and especially asymmetries between language varieties, help reinforce negative stereotypes about individuals identified on the basis of racial, social, and/or ethnic characteristics. However, before discussing the work of Hymes and Labov, I want to recognize the relevance of Karl Marx in this discussion because of his commitment (with Engels) to understand how market economies help establish and fortify social relations in all aspects of life, and to demonstrate some of the alienating effects of the accumulation and distribution of capital on the human condition.

Marx and Political Economy

Karl Marx famously wrote: "If everything were as it appeared on the surface, there would be no need for science" (cited in Harvey 2014, p. 4). While Marx claimed that our task should be to change the world rather than to understand it, he also realized early on that it was necessary to spend a great deal of time conducting research in order to explain the principles of capital accumulation and circulation in order to understand and explain social relations under so-called free market economies. Marx used the term 'fetishism' to refer to the masks, disguises, and distortions that surround us, and his desire to understand what was *really* going on in the world, especially with reference to the nature and effects of rapid industrialization in nineteenth-century Europe, required a massive analysis and critique of capital in order to uncover the fundamental bases of social relations and social inequality that he, and many others, were all too aware of. In volume 1 of his magisterial work *Capital* (1867/1967), Marx made the following observation regarding the task that confronted the reader of his book:

> The method of analysis which I have employed, and which had not previously been applied to economic subjects, makes the reading of the first chapters rather arduous ... That is a disadvantage I am powerless to overcome, unless it be by forewarning and forearming those readers who zealously seek the truth. *There is no royal road to science, and only those who do not dread the fatiguing climb of its steep paths have a chance of gaining its luminous summits.* (Capital, vol. 1, p. 21 [italics are added]; cited in Harvey [2006, p. 1])

While Marx and Engel's work on political economy is relevant for the understanding and interpretation of concepts that will be discussed in this book, including the 'de-skilling' of refugees in the Canadian labor market and monopolistic protectionist policies in many skilled professions, the key insight of relevance is that Marx penetrated surface phenomena (including 'fetishes') in order to provide a systematic explanation for the social and economic inequalities he observed in nineteenth-century England and Europe.[2] Although the circumstances and histories of many (but not all) newcomers who arrive in Canada in the twenty-first century are quite different from those that characterized industrializing Europe in the nineteenth century, there are similarities as well; while England had a long history of class-based social and economic stratification, reinforced and exacerbated by the rapid expansion and domestication of skilled labor in the service of capital, in Canada, immigrants with postsecondary education and relevant work experience, although relatively better positioned than nineteenth-century British laborers with regard to working conditions and access to social services, including health care, still face challenges to compete in an economy marked by constant changes in the types of skills workers need, including the ability to learn and adapt to ever-changing advances in technology, constant reorganization of the workplace, and changing demands placed on all categories of workers. Obsolescence and structural unemployment of both unskilled and skilled labor have long been features, indeed driving forces, of the industrialized capitalist system from its earliest days (Montgomery 1987), and are no less pervasive in the globalized knowledge economy of the twenty-first century. Therefore, although there are particular facts that render the Canadian context different from that of the United States and other industrialized countries, there are fundamental similarities that apply to market societies, generally, extending well into the past.

It is difficult, if not impossible, to define immigrants as a class in the same way that Marx identified 'workers,' 'capitalists,' and the 'bourgeoisie' for analytic purposes in his theoretical analysis of capital. The most relevant commonality for the purposes of this discussion is that first-generation immigrants (and I include refugees in the category 'immigrant' throughout the discussion in this chapter), by definition, were born somewhere else and are not (yet) Canadian citizens (this definition would exclude, for example, a person born of Canadian parents in the United States who grew up in the United States and then moved to Canada as an adult, among other scenarios that can easily be imagined). Beyond that basic commonality, the nature and degree of 'foreignness' of an immigrant (whether first generation or subsequent Canadian-born generation) can be understood in a number of ways, most especially, in terms of apparent and ascribed racial, linguistic, religious, and cultural characteristics, along with indices of cultural capital, such as level of education, professional training, and work experience recent immigrants obtained in their country of origin. Given the wide range of personal characteristics recent immigrants possess, it is dangerous to make any generalizations as to the likelihood they will (or won't) eventually be 'successfully integrated' into Canadian society, assuming that integration is their goal in moving to Canada (which it may not be). Yet, aggregate data (described in the first chapter) provide strong evidence that recent immigrants (this includes refugees) are less likely to be employed in the professions they practiced in their country of origin, that their rates of unemployment will be higher, and that their earnings will be lower (controlling for education) than comparable Canadian cohorts, among other important differences. Many explanations are offered to account for these facts, including lack of 'Canadian work experience,' non-native language skills in English or French, lack of 'appropriate' sociocultural sensitivities (i.e., not being able to 'behave' the way Canadians are expected to behave), among other explanations.[3] While these explanations may have merit in some cases, they are not adequate to account for the overall outcomes experienced by the most well-educated and professionally credentialed immigrants over the past 25 years.

In order to properly interpret these attested facts in the Canadian context, it is necessary to consider both quantitative data (such as rates of (un) employment, underemployment, earnings, wealth disparities, gender biases, and other available demographic classifications, cross-tabulated [where information is available] with immigrant class, national origin, race/ethnicity, religious affiliation, and language competencies), and qualitative data, mainly through the investigation of the lives of affected individuals through case studies, the focus of research in this book. A theoretical framework that has been used in research in Europe, Canada, and other contexts to describe the array of factors that correlate with poverty and other indices of socioeconomic marginalization of people in democratic 'advanced' societies is *social exclusion* (Good Gingrich 2003a, 2003b). Lightman and Good Gingrich (2012, p. 124) define social exclusion as "the official procedures and everyday practices that function to (re) produce and justify economic, spatial, socio-political, and subjective divides ... The outcomes of social exclusion are secured through the denial of legitimate means of accumulating various types of capital from subordinate social positions. Social exclusion denies effective exchange of one's holdings—or capability—and thus cuts off avenues for upward mobility." The authors consider social exclusion to be a dynamic process that cannot be adequately understood solely as data measured at points in time; rather, their approach recognizes the shifting nature of the codes of differentiation and schemes of valuation (p. 124).

In Chap. 1, I provided an example of how the concept of social exclusion can be applied in the case of International Medical Graduates (IMGs) in the province of Alberta; IMGs who are fully qualified to practice medicine in their countries of origin are denied entry to the profession in Canada because they are placed in a category (IMG) created to differentiate them as being in a subordinate/unequal position relative to physicians with medical degrees acquired in Canada or in other Anglophone countries (Canadian-born persons who obtain their medical degree in other countries are also categorized as IMG, although they may have certain advantages if, for instance, they are native English speakers and not visible minorities); a quota system, along with language requirements (in English) that are unrealistic and not particularly relevant in the practice of medicine, renders their training and capabilities as nontransferable to Canada unless they undergo an expensive and lengthy retraining that is beyond the reach of most IMGs, and which may or may not result in certification by national and/or provincial governing bodies (see Wass et al. 2003 and Roberts et al. 2000, which investigate the effects of ethnicity on the evaluation of physicians in the United Kingdom). Other research (e.g., Krahn et al. 2000) has documented a range of barriers across Canada that pose often insurmountable barriers to professional accreditation for immigrants. However, the effects of social exclusion through barriers to professional accreditation is only one example of how social exclusion diminishes possibilities for upward mobility for refugees and other classes of immigrants in Canada. Another example that illustrates the workings of social exclusion is the way that bureaucracies and social policies create barriers that cannot be overcome because they are obscure, unevenly applied, and/or counterproductive to the ends they are designed to achieve. An example is revealed in an interview with members of the Somali family in Phase II of our project. Aziza (a pseudonym), the 58-year-old single mother of a family of one daughter and two sons (living together in Calgary), and two sons still living in Somalia, had been trying for some time to sponsor her two sons in Somalia to move to Canada; however, the government imposed conditions that were impossible for her to meet, as we will see in a portion of the transcribed interview on October 23, 2010, below. Full-time employment is a prerequisite for sponsorship, yet prospective employers require her to work during the time she is taking government-subsidized LINC ESL classes; thus, Aziza cannot get a job, due in part to her lack of English proficiency, but also because prospective employers demand she be available during the hours she is learning English; furthermore, her attempts to reunite her two sons in Somalia with her family in Canada have been repeatedly thwarted, despite promises made to her by the Canadian government *before* she immigrated to Canada (translated from Somali):

Aziza: *Before I was brought to Canada, the government told me that I would get the help necessary to settle in Canada and that my children will be brought to Canada since they live in a war-torn country and their father was killed. I would like to know what happened to that promise. I will learn the answer in the future, God willing. One of the things that life in Canada is becoming meaningless for me is that my dream to reunite with my children and see all of my children in one house is in limbo. The last time I have been to the immigration office, I was told that they (her sons) are not considered family members since they passed 18 years of age. So the promise made yesterday seems to be nullified today or truth has become a thing of the past; I don't really understand what is happening. The government told me something. I was brought to this country. I requested to sponsor my children which I told them before I came. I was waiting for that to happen. And now the process goes back to square one. They are not considered family members. Another one is, you have to have a full-time job. I don't speak the language so I have to go to school to learn the language. When you look for a job, you are denied because of language or they ask you to quit school.*

> *The whole thing is very complex. I don't understand. It is either one of two things: we haven't gotten enough information about the system in Canada yet or maybe the government behaves like this.* (Interview October 23, 2010)

I could provide dozens of other examples from stories told to us by members of the six families we interviewed in Phase II of the project that demonstrate frustrations with government bureaucracy resulting in long wait times and contradictory information provided; the stories of the family members recounted in Chaps. 4 and 5 of this book provide ample additional examples. Native-born citizens in Canada and the United States have also experienced the delays, obfuscations, and frustrating encounters with impersonal bureaucracies, including unreasonable and changing criteria to obtain necessary documents, licenses, permits, and so on; in the case of vulnerable populations (both native-born citizens and noncitizen refugees), the ability to effectively cope with such issues is diminished because the ability to access the tools necessary to deal with obstacles is restricted; people with financial means can hire attorneys, they (or their representatives) can more effectively communicate with government bureaucracies and demand results in a language and discourse style they command. In short, individuals with the 'right' social and cultural capital, including financial means and appropriate language skills, are more empowered to *change* their situation for the better; assertion of individual agency is not sufficient *in itself* to overcome the layers of obstacles that are faced by many immigrants; in the case of refugee immigrants, who generally have fewer financial resources and lower levels of proficiency in the dominant language (English, in the case of Canada outside Quebec), compared to other classes of immigrants, the challenges can be overwhelming.

In terms of public perceptions and narratives regarding both the welcoming nature of Canadian society and the commitment to the multicultural 'mosaic' image that many Canadians share, there is clearly a disconnect between that image and the actual experiences of many newcomers to Canada. Most of the refugees we interviewed commented favorably on their perception of Canada *before they arrived* as a welcoming country that respected cultural diversity, human rights, and the rule of law. However, the views of many had changed after they arrived in Canada as they came to realize that they were not able to achieve the life they had dreamed about obtaining when they were applying for refugee status. Respect for human rights and the rule of law were features of Canada that were widely affirmed and appreciated by the refugees we interviewed; however, their paths toward social integration[4] were often more difficult than they had anticipated they would be. The nature of some of those difficulties will be taken up in Chaps. 4 and 5.

There is, apparently, broad public support for the view that immigration is necessary and beneficial for the Canadian economy. Reitz (2012, p. 522) provides results from Gallup Polls in Canada that show "... that over the period 1975–2005, in every year but one (1982, a recession year), a majority of the population has either supported immigration levels or has wanted them increased." Satzewich (2015, p. 60) argues that since Confederation (1867), Canadian immigration policy has been guided by the goals of economic development and social reproduction: "... the prevailing political consensus is that various types of immigrants help drive economic development because they are a source of labour for employers and of innovation and capital for small and large businesses." With regard to social reproduction, according to the goals of Canada's immigration and refugee policies stipulated in the Immigration and Refugee Protection Act (2001), item 3.(1)(b), one of the objectives of the Act is "to enrich and strengthen the social and cultural fabric of Canadian society, while respecting the federal, bilingual and multicultural character of Canada" (in Satzewich 2015, p. 248). The wording here seems to suggest that the 'social and cultural fabric of Canadian society' is something known (but not specified) and that fundamental to that 'fabric' is official bilingualism (English and French) and multiculturalism. One can wonder about what is meant by the words "while respecting ..." which seem to suggest that the 'social and cultural fabric of Canadian society' is either self-evident or the reader can supply the shared (assumed) meaning of that 'fabric,' which is really a euphemism for Canadian national identity.[5] It seems that for most Canadians, immigrants are necessary for sustaining and expanding the Canadian economy; whether Canadian society supports changes to the character of the white European-based settler nation that was confederated in 1867 to a truly multicultural/multiracial/multilingual nation *not* based exclusively upon a white European normative ethnic and linguistic identity is another matter altogether (Bannerji 2000). In fact, the idea of 'multicultural Canada' is a relatively new construct that was first officially enunciated by the federal government as a formal policy in 1971. Critics of the Canadian policy of multiculturalism (e.g., Haque 2012; Ricento 2017) point out that the impetus for the original Canadian Multiculturalism policy of 1971 was a weak and politically expedient response to complaints from 'other' groups not dealt with in the Official Languages Act (1969) that established English and French as the two official languages (and 'races') of Canada. That policy came about as a pragmatic response to the threat to national unity posed by political forces in the province of Quebec, promulgated by the 'Quiet Revolution' of the 1960s and culminating in the passage of the Official Languages Act in 1969. The well-documented history surrounding the Royal Commission on Bilingualism and Biculturalism (B & B Commission, 1963–1969), whose recommendations led to passage of the Official Languages Act in 1969, makes clear that the purpose of the commission was preordained by the mandate given by the Lester B. Pearson government, which stated that the commission was to:

> Inquire into and report upon the existing state of bilingualism and biculturalism in Canada and to recommend what steps should be taken to develop the Canadian Confederation on the basis of *an equal partnership between the two founding races...* [italics added]

As Haque (2012) notes, the commission was limited in the scope and goals of their work to the interests, concerns, and aspirations of the two 'founding races,' Anglophones and Francophones, and not on the interests and claims to equal national standing of 'other' ethnolinguistic/ethnocultural groups, such as immigrants and Indigenous peoples (FNMI: First Nations, Métis, Inuit). Even today, as Haque (p. 18) notes, "... membership in the Canadian nation is achieved through designation into one of four groups: English, French, Aboriginal, and 'Multicultural,'" where multicultural has come to mean 'cultures and languages other than English and French,' an undifferentiated category of 'other' groups. Indigenous peoples, whose long presence on the North American continent should have qualified them as 'founding races,' with coequal status with the English and the French, were argued to have no coherence because of the many languages that were spoken among the various tribes.[6] Haque notes that the 'problems' of the Indigenous groups were viewed as 'unique,' requiring further study, an approach, Haque notes (2012, p. 79) "... that served not only to peripheralize but also to pathologize them." Their marginal status was quite literally represented by the lack of space given to them in the preliminary report of the B & B Commission, a short paragraph in the instructions given for preparing briefs for the commission (p. 79).

Thus, while Canada is a liberal democratic state in terms of its political and institutional structures, especially given its status as a Constitutional Confederation with a Charter of Rights and Freedoms, it also has a history that includes policies designed to keep racialized 'others' and their non-colonial languages out of Canada,[7] the denial of basic human rights and liberties to Indigenous and some immigrant groups, along with the granting of privileged 'special' status to the two 'Founding Races'—Anglophones and Francophone (or, the English and the French); the dissonance between at least some of the language of what the Canadian nation 'ought' to be, stipulated in the Charter of Rights and Freedoms (1982), and the well-documented 'is' of the marginalization and denial of rights to a variety of indigenous and immigrant groups based on ethnicity, race, gender, national origin, culture, language, and/or religion (resulting in social exclusion) renders the mosaic a 'crazy quilt' of mixed messages with clearly demarcated 'firm' lines around various sections of the quilt. Therefore, it is reasonable to look 'beneath the surface' of government statistics and popular narratives on the nature of Canadian 'multicultural' society and seek additional perspectives to account for the disparate outcomes of certain groups (e.g., immigrants/refugees, among others). Certainly, one way to evaluate the 'Canadian promise' of equal opportunity and access to the same rights, goods, economic opportunities, and social services that native-born, White Canadians tend to enjoy[8] is to provide the opportunity for immigrants (and specifically refugees in this book) to talk about their own experiences since arriving in Canada, and this is precisely the rationale for our research project and the rationale for sharing those results in this book. To paraphrase Marx, public (and especially political) discourses on the situation in Canada with regard to the status of immigrants should not be taken at face value; following Marx, we need to be skeptical of what 'appears on the surface' and be open to understandings that might contradict the comforting 'official' narrative that is partial and often distorted.

How Language Is Organized as a Human Problem and Resource

I now turn to two scholars of more recent vintage than Marx whose commitment to understanding human society has, as with Marx, been strongly motivated by humanistic values; just as Marx was ultimately interested in understanding the causes of—and remedies for—human alienation[9] in his analysis of political economy (*Economic and Philosophic Manuscripts of 1844*), Dell Hymes and William Labov developed theoretical and methodological tools in order to understand the ways that language is organized as a human problem and resource, and to identify the links between language and systems of domination and subordination in order to advocate for social justice for marginalized communities. Since an important thesis of this book is that language is very often a barrier to 'becoming Canadian,' and that language is generally associated with ethnicity, race, and other affiliations that tend to marginalize individuals into particular classes, or groups (Ricento 2014), the work and views of Hymes and Labov are of particular relevance.

Dell Hymes' attraction to linguistic anthropology informed his commitment to social justice, and he was from the beginning of his career interested in understanding the relationship between language and systems of domination and subordination. As is the case with intellectuals who change the way we think about the world, Hymes was not constrained by existing disciplinary boundaries or orthodoxies. Alan Luke, in his introduction to an anthology of Hymes' work, *Ethnography, Linguistics, Narrative Inequality: Toward an Understanding of Voice* (1996, p. vii), notes that Hymes' broader proposal was for a science of 'mediative' practice, involving *interventions with, on behalf of and alongside of marginalized communities of speakers* (italics added). In Hymes' essay "Speech and Language: On the Origins and Foundations of Inequality Among Speakers," originally published in 1973 in the journal *Daedalus*, he explains his justification for a 'mediative' as opposed to an 'extractive,' ethnography of language that is a science of activism and intervention:

> In this way one can go beyond a liberal humanism that merely recognizes the abstract potentiality of all languages, to a humanism which can deal with concrete situations, with *the inequalities that actually obtain, and help to transform them through knowledge of the ways in which language is actually organized as a human problem and resource.* (italics added)

From these interests and concerns, Hymes, along with John Gumperz and other colleagues developed an 'ethnography of communication' that remains influential to the present day, and which informs the research project I will be discussing in this book. In Chaps. 4 and 6, I will provide concrete examples that demonstrate how inequalities are enacted in English language programs for immigrants and refugees.

William Labov, a pioneer in what came to be known as Variationist Sociolinguistics (1966), played an important role in advancing social justice by using the tools of linguistic analysis to demystify 'common sense' views about the supposed linguistic and cognitive deficits of African Americans living in American inner cities. In a classic essay "The Logic of Nonstandard English" (1972), Labov debunked the Verbal Deprivation Theory promoted by psychologists (e.g., Bereiter and Engelmann 1966) which claimed, among other things, that African American children in the United States come to school without sufficient verbal ability to succeed. Bereiter and Engelmann (1966, pp. 112–113), based on a study of four-year-old Black children from Urbana, Illinois, claimed that the children's communication was by gestures, "single words," and "a series of badly connected words or phrases." The researchers described the children's speech as "the language of culturally deprived children ... [that] is not merely an underdeveloped version of standard English, but is a basically non-logical mode of expressive behavior." Labov successfully and powerfully argued that the idea of verbal deprivation has no basis in social reality, that Black children in the urban ghettos receive a lot of verbal stimulation, and participate in a highly verbal culture. He claimed that the psychologists' lack of understanding of linguistics along with poor experimental design and methodology resulted in a fundamental misreading and misinterpretation of the verbal abilities of Black children. The key point here is that research in the 1960s by some psychologists (e.g., Bereiter and Engelmann 1966; Jensen 1969) and sociologists (e.g., Basil Bernstein 1966) placed the blame for school failure on minority children who were (mis)characterized as having a variety of cognitive deficits, especially with regard to their language abilities. Other researchers (including Labov) located the problem not in the children but in the relations between them and the school system. This work stimulated research by other scholars in the social sciences to examine the nature and impact of ideologies about language on social practices and policies, and how these ideologies impacted the school experiences of different groups defined in terms of socioeconomic status, ethnicity, race, and/or language or language variety spoken.[10] Labov's work was crucial in showing how social scientists' presumptive theories and research methods can be ill-informed and inappropriate for the contexts for which they are used, and that published findings based on those ill-informed presumptions can have serious consequences on the life chances of individuals from minority communities, whether they be linguistic, racial, or ethnic minorities. The published findings of the psychologists who espoused the Verbal Deprivation Theory *did* provide 'scientific' reasons for blaming the victim for his or her academic failings, and helped to justify and validate existing, long-standing societal discrimination toward the minorities in question. A progressive view on the advances that can be made in science, a view I embrace and one that is not in favor or in step with at least some postmodern theories, validates the research conducted by Labov as both advancing our *understanding* of human verbal behavior while also *advancing the principles* of research ethics that Labov elaborated in 1982[11]; that is, Labov's science supersedes that of Bereiter and Engelmann, because it debunked a 'common sense' belief with regard to the purported linguistic and cognitive deficiencies of African American youth, while also focusing attention onto an education system ill-prepared and unwilling to recognize and validate the legitimacy of African American Vernacular English (AAVE) necessary to ensure that speakers of 'nonstandard' varieties of English (such as AAVE) would have equal access to the school curriculum via the 'standard' English that was a second dialect for speakers of AAVE (Rickford 1999). The work of Hymes and Labov helps us better understand the nature and causes of, and possible ways to ameliorate, societal inequalities and injustices, an approach that I aspire to and applied in my investigation of the situation of refugees in Canada. This deeper understanding is especially relevant to interpreting the experiences of members of the Martinez family (Chap. 4) and Patrick and Chantal (Chap. 5) with regard to their experiences as 'visible' minorities whose language repertoires defined them in ways that reduced their ability to obtain the appropriate education and employment opportunities that would have improved their current and future lives in Canada. The experiences of these individuals, and others we interviewed in Phase II of the project, provide clear evidence that their status as refugees, with limited financial and social resources, with limited English proficiency, and as visible racial/ethnic minorities often placed them in subordinate positions vis-à-vis individuals and institutions that negatively impacted their ability to achieve their stated goal of integrating into Canadian society.

The Moral and Ethical Responsibilities of the Researcher

Both Hymes and Labov (in step with Marx) understood that views on the 'social order' are often based on 'common sense' understandings of the 'world,' understandings that reflect the beliefs and prejudices, the ideologies and self-interest of groups (including academic researchers) who benefit from and, therefore, conform to existing sociopolitical and socioeconomic systems[12]; even when scholars *claim* their work serves the interests and goals of 'social justice,' the concept of social justice itself is often fuzzy and under-specified, often paternalistic, partial, and shallow, and is usually not based on a systematic analysis that *should* critically address the nature and role of political economy, historical factors, and the education establishment that employs these scholars.

The work and views of Marx, Hymes, and Labov were discussed in order to illustrate how research in the social sciences (theoretical and applied) can and, in fact, should be scientifically rigorous, creative, and ethical, while being responsive to social conditions and systemic relations that are inimical to human flourishing and societal well-being, as understood by those conducting research. Such understanding is not easily gained, nor is it dependent on or derived from a fixed, objective view on what constitutes 'human flourishing,' nor is there an a priori road map or 'tool box' of theories and methods that are likely to point us in the right direction, nor is there any way to be certain that our tools of analysis are the best, or most appropriate, for the questions we are inclined to ask; at a very minimum, persons who claim to be doing research must be aware of and pay attention to how their research cannot be neutral with regard to its potential impact on the lives of people and on society, in general, and therefore they should have a basis to believe that their research will be of some benefit to human society, or at least be consistent with some reasonably articulated moral framework, even though the researcher is not in a position to know how his or her findings will be taken up and used by interested parties over time. These views and comments are aptly summarized by Noam Chomsky (cited in Barsky 1997, p. 141) who said: "people have a responsibility for the foreseeable consequences of their actions, and therefore have the responsibility of thinking about the research they undertake and what it might lead to under existing conditions." I have tried to be responsible in conducting research that focuses on issues that should be of concern to Canadians and citizens of other countries because how these issues are understood (or ignored) by the general public will influence whether, and to what degree, politicians and political leaders will respond to them. I hope that the evidence presented in this book will contribute to national conversations on how *all* Canadians can help promote the full *integration* of immigrants and refugees in all aspects of national life.

Notes

1. For a recent comprehensive and thorough treatment of the evolution of disciplinary knowledge in the physical and biological sciences, social sciences, and humanities over the past 150 years, I highly recommend Harvey Graff's (2015) book *Undisciplining Knowledge: Interdisciplinarity in the Twentieth Century.*
2. The best and most comprehensive treatment of Marx's political-economic thought is David Harvey's *The Limits to Capital* (2006). Another more recent work by Harvey (*Seventeen Contradictions and the End of Capitalism*, 2014) is less technical and more accessible than the 2006 book.
3. The lack of recognition of foreign-earned academic and professional credentials is an undeniable barrier to labor force integration, especially for those immigrants from non-Anglophone and developing countries.
4. Robinson (1998, p. 118) argues that "integration is a chaotic concept: a word used by many but understood differently by most … a concept that is individualized, contested and contextual."
5. The effect of Official Bilingualism has been to marginalize the status and utility of non-official languages (including Aboriginal languages) in public life (Ricento 2013), and the goal of multiculturalism policy has not been to support and fortify 'other' cultures in any meaningful way, since the goal of government policies has been the total assimilation of immigrants into 'mainstream' Canadian official languages and cultural values (assumed, but widely shared).
6. In a report commissioned by the B & B Commission, "Indians and Eskimos of Canada: An Overview of Studies of Relevance to the Royal Commission on Bilingualism and Biculturalism" (Vallee 1966), the author argued that people of Indian and Eskimo ancestry could not be considered an ethnic group: "One reason that we cannot consider the people of Indian and Eskimo ancestry as an ethnic group equivalent, say, to the French-Canadian, English-Canadian, Ukrainian-Canadian, and the like, is that there is no one language which serves as a symbol of distinctive identity at the national level. Students of language classify Indian languages into lin-

guistic groups or stocks ... For Canada, such a classification yields ten Indian and one Eskimo language groups or stocks" (Vallee 1966, p. 68).

7. Ball (2015, p. 180) provides examples of such policies; these include "... the Chinese Exclusion Act of 1923, elements of which persisted until 1967, the Continuous Passage Act from 1908-47, designed to prevent non-European immigrants from other British colonies, especially a perceived 'Hindu invasion', and the similar, present-day Safe Third Country Agreement, enacted in 2004, designed to keep out refugee claimants who have passed through another potentially safe country en route to Canada." Religious orders, for example, the Doukhobors, Hutterites, and Mennonites were prohibited from entering Canada at various times in the nineteenth and twentieth centuries (Knowles 2007). During World Wars I and II, German, Ukrainian, Italian, and Japanese Canadians were moved from their homes to internment camps in rural areas; after the bombing of Pearl Harbor in 1941, 22,000 Japanese Canadians were stripped of their property and sent to live in detention campus in British Columbia or to other provinces to work as manual laborers on sugar beet farms. At the termination of the war, more than 10,500 Japanese were pressured into leaving for Japan under a 'repatriation' program (Knowles 2007).
8. It is not just immigrants who have fallen behind in Canada; as Lightman and Good Gingrich (2012, p. 125) note, "... the gap between Canada's rich and poor not only persists, but has increased more rapidly than ever in the past three decades" (Fortin et al. 2012; Osberg 2008; Yalnizyan 2009). Since the mid-1990s, both inequality in household earnings and numbers of people living in poverty have risen faster in Canada than in any other OECD country (OECD 2008). In 2008, "after a decade of blockbuster economic growth and job creation," there were 2.2 million working-age adults living in poverty in Canada (Yalnizyan 2009, pp. 4–5). Since the early 1980s, the share of low-wage jobs (less than $10/hour) has not decreased, and increases in the average wage of full-time workers have not even kept pace with inflation (Saunders 2005; Yalnizyan 2009). The result is a net decline in standard of living for the majority of Canadians.
9. Marx reinterpreted alienation as it was previously conceived by Hegel as a problem not to be overcome in thought, but by action. For Marx, "Alienation is estrangement from our human nature; the essence of human nature is our character as social and productive creatures who create social relations as well as material objects, relationships that under the right conditions are fruitful and life enhancing, and under the wrong conditions oppressive and destructive. The concept of alienation is an all-purpose critical tool to illuminate the ways in which developed modern societies ... set us at odds with one another, with our work, and with our own deepest natures" (Ryan 2012, p. 777).

10. Another early landmark study was conducted by Ray Rist (1970) who, in a two-and-one-half-year longitudinal study of a single group of African American kindergarten children, found that the teacher (herself African American) developed expectations of the academic potential and abilities of each student based on her subjective evaluation of that student's oral language.
11. Labov (1982, p. 173) proposed four principles that should be adhered to by researchers; two of these speak directly to researcher ethics:

Principle of error correction: A scientist who becomes aware of a widespread idea or social practice with important consequences that is invalidated by his own data is obligated to bring this error to the attention of the widest possible audience (p. 172)

Principle of debt incurred: An investigator who has obtained linguistic data from members of a speech community has an obligation to use the knowledge based on that data for the benefit of the community.

These two principles strongly influence the choices that I made with regard to why I decided to collaborate with particular refugee families, how I conducted the research, and what uses I have made and will continue to make of the outcomes of the research, in terms of dissemination and reciprocity with the individuals and institutions I have collaborated with throughout the project.

12. As Hymes (1985, p. vii) notes: "Were there no political domination or social stratification in the world, there would still be linguistic inequality … Allocation and hierarchy are intrinsic. Nor should the investments of many, perhaps even including ourselves, in some existing arrangements be underestimated. Effective change in the direction of greater equality will only partly be change in attitude, or removal of external domination; it will be inseparable in many cases from change of social system."

References

Ball, J. (2015). Trouble on the frontier: The perils of persisting colonial language policies in Canada. In A. Yiakoumetti (ed.), *Multilingualism and Language Education: Sociolinguistic and Pedagogical Perspectives from Commonwealth Countries* (pp. 177–198). Cambridge: Cambridge University Press.

Bannerji, H. (2000). *The dark side of the nation: Essays on multiculturalism, nationalism, and gender.* Toronto: Canadian Scholars' Press.

Barsky, R.F. (1997). *Noam Chomsky: A life of dissent.* Cambridge, MA: MIT Press.

Bereiter, C. and Engelmann, S. (1966). *Teaching disadvantaged children in the pre-school.* Englewood Cliffs, NJ: Prentice-Hall.

Bernstein, B. (1966). Elaborated and restricted codes: Their social origins and some consequences. In J. Gumperz and D. Hymes (eds.), *The ethnography of communication, American Anthropologist* 66 (no. 6, part 2).

Fortin, N., Green, D.A., Lemieux, T., Milligan, K. and Craig Riddell, W. (2012). Issues and commentaries. Canadian inequality: Recent developments and policy options. *Canadian Public Policy* XXXVIII. 2, 121–145.

Good Gingrich, L. (2003a). Social exclusion as an individual kind—A categorical point of view. *Canadian Review of Social Policy* Fall/Winter 52, 93–115.

Good Gingrich, L. (2003b). Theorizing social exclusion: Determinants, mechanisms, dimensions, forms, and acts of resistance. In W. Shera (ed.), *Emerging perspectives on anti-oppressive practice* (pp. 3–23). Toronto: Canadian Scholar's Press, Inc./Women's Press.

Graff, H. (2015). *Undisciplining knowledge: Interdisciplinarity in the Twentieth Century.* Baltimore: Johns Hopkins University Press.

Haque, E. (2012). *Multiculturalism within a bilingual framework: Language, race, and belonging in Canada.* Toronto: University of Toronto Press.

Harvey, D. (2006). *The limits to capital.* London: Verso.

Harvey, D. (2014). *Seventeen contradictions and the end of capitalism.* New York: Oxford University Press.

Hymes, D. (1985). Preface. In N. Wolfson and J. Manes (Eds.), *Language of inequality* (pp. v–viii). Berlin: Mouton.

Hymes, D. (1996). *Ethnography, linguistics, narrative inequality: Toward an understanding of voice.* London: Taylor & Francis.

Jensen, A. (1969). How much can we boost IQ and scholastic achievement? *Harvard Educational Review* 39, 1–123.

Johnson, D.C. (2016). Theoretical foundations. In E. Barakos & J.W. Unger (eds.), *Discursive approaches to language policy* (pp. 11–21). London: Palgrave Macmillan.

Knowles, V. (2007). *Strangers at our gates: Canadian immigration and immigration policy, 1540–2006* (Rev. Ed.). Toronto: Dundurn Press.

Krahn, H., Derwing, T., Mulder, M., and Wilkinson, L. (2000). Educated and underemployed: Refugee integration into the Canadian Labour Market. *Journal of International Migration and Integration* 1 (1), 59–84.

Labov, W. (1966/2006). *The social stratification of English in New York City* (second edition). New York: Cambridge University Press.

Labov, W. (1972). The logic of nonstandard English. In *Language in the inner city: Studies in the Black English vernacular* (chapter 5). Philadelphia, PA: University of Pennsylvania Press.

Labov, W. (1982). Objectivity and commitment in linguistic science: The case of the Black English trial in Ann Arbor. *Language in Society* 11(2), 165–201.

Lightman, N. and Good Gingrich, L. (2012). The intersecting dynamics of social exclusion: Age, gender, race and immigrant status in Canada's labour market. *Canadian Ethnic Studies*, 44 (3), 121–145.

Marx, K. (1884/1964). *The economic and philosophic manuscripts of 1844*. New York: International Publishers.

Marx, K. (1867/1967). *Capital*. New York: International Publishers.

Montgomery, D. (1987). *The fall of the house of labor: The workplace, the state, and American labor activism, 1865–1925*. Cambridge: Cambridge University Press.

OECD. (2008). Growing unequal? Income distribution and poverty in OECD countries. Paris: OECD.

Osberg, L. (2008). *A quarter century of economic inequality in Canada: 1981–2006*. Toronto: Canadian Centre for Policy Alternatives.

Reitz, J.G. (2012). The distinctiveness of Canadian immigration experience. *Patterns of Prejudice* 46 (5), 518–538.

Ricento, T. (2013). The consequences of official bilingualism on the status and perception of non-official languages in Canada. *Journal of Multilingual and Multicultural Development*, 34 (5), 475–489.

Ricento, T. (2014). Thinking about language: What political theorists need to know about language in the real world. *Language Policy* 13 (4), 351–369

Ricento, T. (2015). Foreword. In F. Hult and D.C. Johnson (eds.), *Research methods in language policy and planning: A practical guide*, (pp. xii–xiv). Malden, MA: Wiley Blackwell.

Ricento, T. (2017). Conceptualizing language: Linguistic theory and language policy. In H. Peukert, T. Hagen, and I. Gogolin (Eds.), *Dynamics of Linguistic Diversity*, (pp. 13–29). Amsterdam: John Benjamins.

Rickford, J. (1999). *African American Vernacular English: Features, evolution, educational implications*. Oxford: Blackwell.

Rist, R. (1970). Student social class and teacher expectations: The self-fulfilling prophecy in ghetto education. *Harvard Educational Review* 40, 411–451.

Roberts, C., Sarangi, S. Southgate, L., Wakeford, R. and Wass, V. (2000). Oral Examinations: Equal Opportunities, Ethnicity, and Fairness in the MRCGP. *British Medical Journal*, Vol. 320, No. 7231 (Feb. 5, 2000), 370–374. URL: http://www.jstor.org/stable/25187083

Robinson, V. (1998). Defining and measuring successful refugee integration. In *Proceedings of ECRE international conference on integration of refugees in Europe*. Antwerp, Brussels: ECRE, November 1998.

Ryan, A. (2012). *On politics: Book two: A history of political thought: Hobbes to the present*. New York: Liveright.

Satzewich, V. (2015). *Points of entry: How Canada's immigration officers decide who gets in*. Vancouver: UBC Press.

Saunders, R. (2005). *Does a rising tide lift all boats? Low paid workers in Canada*. Ottawa: Canadian Policy Research Networks Inc.

Vallee, F.G. (1966). *Indians and Eskimos of Canada: An overview of studies of relevance to the Royal Commission on Bilingualism and Biculturalism*. s.l.: s.n. Amicus number 12033571.

Wass, V., Roberts, C., Hoogenboom, R. Jones, R. and Van der Vleuten, C. (2003). Effect of ethnicity on performance in a final objective structured clinical examination: Qualitative and quantitative study. *British Medical Journal*, Vol. 326, No. 7393 (Apr. 12, 2003), pp. 800–803. URL: http://www.jstor.org/stable/25454174

Yalnizyan, A. (2009). *Shaping a future for everyone: Income inequality not sustainable economically for any of us*. Ottawa: Canadian Centre for Policy Alternatives.

CHAPTER 3

The Study

Abstract In this chapter, I provide detailed information on the research project 'Linguistic and Cultural Barriers to Refugees' access to medical and social services' in Calgary (2009–2011) for which I was the principal investigator. Detailed information on the refugee families that participated in the study are provided, as well as information on the methodology used and information on the findings obtained. A total of 30 refugee families from the countries Myanmar, Bhutan, Somalia, Afghanistan, Colombia, and the Democratic Republic of the Congo, representing 30 different families and 120 people altogether, speaking at least 7 different languages (Dari, Farsi, French, Karen, Nepali, Somali, and Spanish), comprised the original cohort of participants in the research project.

Keywords LINC program • Refugees in Calgary • Barriers to medical and social services • Profiles on participants • Research protocols

Background to the Study

The motivation for the study 'Linguistic and Cultural Barriers to Refugees' Access to Medical and Social Services' in Calgary that I will be describing in this chapter began with a study, in which I was the principal investigator, on the largest Language Instruction for Newcomers to Canada (LINC) program in Calgary (Ricento et al. 2008). Our team investigated

T. Ricento, *Refugees in Canada*,
https://doi.org/10.1007/978-3-030-76453-1_3

how the LINC program operated in terms of curricular content and program design, classroom materials, instructors' roles and philosophy about teaching English as a Second/Foreign/Additional language, the views of program administrators, and funding structures, among other issues; we also interviewed students in the program and asked them to complete questionnaires (after we obtained their consent) that provided information on the languages they knew, country of origin (and other countries where they might have lived), their educational attainment, previous employment/career before arriving in Calgary, current employment situation, and career goals in Canada, among other information we collected. The findings with regard to their current employment status compared to their previous employment and educational level caught our attention; of the 78 LINC students we surveyed, 65% were unemployed, 29% had a survival job, and only 4% were employed in their desired career field. Of significance is that 54% of the sample are highly educated with 43% reporting postsecondary degrees and 11% reporting graduate training. The average age of the respondents was about 41 years old and 64% were female. In our one-on-one interviews with the students, we found that many believed they would never be able to re-establish their careers in Canada as highly trained professionals. Among the professions identified in our survey were physician, engineer, computer programmer, and physical therapist. Our team decided that we needed to better understand the data that we obtained on the participants in this LINC program. In our review of the published literature, we found that the status of newcomers to Canada with regard to barriers to employment was nothing new; we learned that while it takes a significant amount of time, effort, and money for well-educated foreign-born permanent residents to gain employment and begin to integrate into Canadian society, many succeed in large part because of their willingness to take jobs outside their areas of professional expertise, often for low wages and with little potential for upward mobility, and because they become resigned to the fact that they will likely never have the same occupation and income level they had attained prior to moving to Canada, *despite* the cultural capital they acquired before landing in Canada. In a study funded by Citizenship and Immigration Canada (Abu-Laban et al. 1999), a sample of 616 refugees from managerial and professional occupations, along with skilled trades, accounted for 37% of adult refugee employment, while 32% worked in semi-skilled jobs and 31% in unskilled jobs. The unemployment rate for the refugee men was 14% and 19% for women. Fifty-eight percent considered themselves to be underemployed. Other studies reveal similar patterns of unemployment and underemployment for refugee populations in Canada. Chapter 1 provides an overview of research findings on this point.

The students in the LINC program we investigated arrived through various immigration programs: economic class, family class, and refugee programs; we decided to focus on the experiences of refugees because we found a gap in the research literature on this group, especially on the situation in Calgary. Our review of the literature found that refugees face a number of challenges that are specific to their status as persons fleeing war, persecution, various types of physical abuse, and economic privation. These challenges affect the ability of refugees to find employment, housing, proper medical care and legal advice, support, and adequate services from the schools their children attend. While there are some similarities between refugee and non-refugee immigrants in unemployment rates and availability of language instruction, there are significant differences in the areas of housing, linguistic barriers, experiences of children in schooling, and experiences of women. Pruebber and Tanasescu (2007, p. 8) conducted an informal telephone survey to find out which groups were using housing assistance and services in Canada, and the challenges faced by immigrants (refugee and non-refugee). They note: "[R]esearch based on the Longitudinal Survey of Immigrants to Canada and Census 2001 has demonstrated that the social networks of newcomers and greater tendency to live in larger family units have helped groups access housing despite a higher incidence of poverty and systematic barriers. While the resiliency of social networks has historically helped cushion market fluctuations, the current housing crisis in Calgary is adding immense pressure on newcomers' ability to obtain and maintain housing." Discrimination in rental housing and shelter agencies contributes to homelessness. Discrimination on the part of landlords takes various forms: refusal to accept money from welfare to pay the rent, no children policy, requirement of a financial premium for access, rent advances, and a requirement of credit history. Refugees are more likely to experience "secondary homelessness," that is, living with friends in crowded or substandard conditions. As many refugees suffer from post-traumatic stress disorder, mainstream shelters can be scary places for them that add to their psychological distress. Many of the refugees who access the shelters are women with children. Balley and Builthuis (2004), based on existing research data, found that refugees are more likely than other classes of immigrants to become homeless. In 2001, 24% of families requiring emergency shelters in Toronto in 1999 were refugee claimants. Workers at homeless shelters are generally trained to work with people with mental health or substance abuse problems, but not necessarily with refugees who have different kinds of problems. The authors recommend better coordination between homeless shelters, settlement agencies, and legal aid services. Schellenberg and Maheux (2007) conducted a longitudinal survey of newcomers to Canada and found that refugees were more likely than family-class immigrants to experience housing problems.

Another similarity between refugees and other categories of immigrants concerns language; while the LINC program does provide basic English instruction, it cannot provide the amount of language instruction necessary to allow immigrants and refugees with technical or professional training to enter the workforce in those professions[1] (leaving aside the issue of barriers to obtaining certification in fields such as medicine, engineering, and education). However, research indicates that refugees face more linguistic barriers compared to economic or family-class immigrants; when asked which was the biggest difficulty experienced in the past four years, 41% of the refugees mentioned linguistic barriers as compared to only 23% of the economic immigrants (Schellenberg and Maheux 2007). Refugees (49%) are more likely than business immigrants (25%) or family-class immigrants (23%) to take at least one language course. Unemployment and inadequate and unaffordable housing clearly have negative impacts on the life experiences of the children of refugees. Refugee claimants in Canada are only eligible for basic social assistance or child tax benefits and emergency health care (not full health coverage). Fantino and Colak (2001) conducted an ethnographic study with ten refugee families in Canada, with a focus on the needs of children. Refugee children present additional problems as compared to immigrant children; many of them have been through war, persecution, refugee camps, killings, torture, and rape. Some have served as soldiers; others have lost their families and everything they knew. Many children go through an extended period of identity confusion. Some refugee parents who also have been traumatized may not offer a healthy psychological environment for their children. Stewart (2008) examined the experiences of high school refugee students in Manitoba who came from countries affected by war. Data consisted of semi-structured interviews, document analysis, and focus group interviews with a total of 51 participants: high school students, school staff members, parents, community members, educational policy makers, social workers, and experts in refugee education. The findings indicate that the post-migration phase is characterized by four categories of barriers to refugee students' progress: educational, economic, environmental, and psychosocial. Refugee students expressed feelings of mistrust and insecurity. Racism, discrimination, and ethnically based conflict were the core themes that emerged from the data collection. Another at-risk component of the refugee population in Canada is that sometimes children are separated from their families. In a study comparing this population in Australia and Canada, Martin and Curran (2007) report that children of all ages are seeking asylum in Canada. In the period January 1, 1999, until September 20, 2002, there were 518 claimants among children aged 0–4, 1051 claimants among children aged 11–15, 1192 claimants among children aged 16–17. This is in contrast to Australia, where the unaccompanied children are generally older.

Finally, Saulnier (2008, p. 27) reports on the experiences of refugee claimant women in Nova Scotia. Based on the experiences reported by these women at a roundtable discussion, it was concluded that refugee women are among the most vulnerable category of immigrants to Canada. They arrive with nothing, many times traumatized, and are forced to face many hardships in Canada and gaps in social services and programs. The author reports that "refugees can be in limbo as claimants for at least a year, and are more likely to be waiting two to three years for a decision, which can either be in their favour or result in deportation."[2]

With these studies and data as starting points, our team developed a series of research strategies and approaches that we felt would help us to gain insights into the actual day-to-day lives of refugees in our local area, Calgary, a city with a population of over one million people. After reviewing the relevant literature and developing a research framework that would require extensive interviews with refugees in Calgary on a range of topics over a period of approximately nine months, we began the process of identifying possible research sites in Calgary. There were several NGOs in Calgary that worked with refugees in various capacities, including providing language instruction, support in locating affordable housing, translation services, counseling, and many other types of support. After interviews with multiple NGOs and social service providers, we were able to establish a relationship with a large center for refugees in Calgary which we will call the Calgary Resettlement Centre (CRC).

The Profile of Refugees in Calgary

After visiting the Calgary Resettlement Centre as a potential research site, postdoctoral research associate Andreea Cervatiuc and I returned and conducted an extensive interview with the Resettlement & Integration Services Coordinator at the CRC (November 6, 2008) for several hours. During the course of the interview, during which the research associate took detailed notes, the coordinator provided her personal views and insights based on her multiple years of experience working in the center. I realize that there is some degree of subjectivity involved in her descriptions; however, her long tenure at the center working with thousands of refugees renders her an expert with 'on the ground' first-person experience. She herself was a refugee from the Middle East and expressed a great deal of empathy and understanding for the people with whom she interacted on a daily basis. What follows are some of her observations on the refugee clients she worked with during their stay at the center and also in follow-up sessions during the months and years after they left the center:

- They come with various levels of education. Some are illiterate.
- Some are single mothers; some have severe emotional problems; some have disabilities.
- Some are isolated and don't go out of the center.
- Counselors at the center try to help grieving refugees open up, but refugees may feel that counselors impose their values on them.
- According to the coordinator, there is variation in the ability of people from different cultural backgrounds to integrate into Canadian society. She claimed that Sudanese integrate better than Ethiopians, and it is difficult for Somalis to settle. Sudanese and Afghanis present particular challenges. The more educated refugees (e.g., Iraqis) have high expectations. Afghanis and Iranians become quite upset when incidents of domestic violence are reported to authorities. Social workers sometimes receive calls from hospitals concerning spousal abuse.

In addition to psychological, social, and cultural differences noted among the refugees from more than 14 countries, the coordinator noted problems with interpretation. At the time of the interview with the coordinator, at least 17 different languages were spoken by refugees at the center: Somali, Arabic, Farsi, Russian, French, Dinka, Spanish, Turkish,

Albanian, Pashto, Urdu, Serbo-Croatian, Polish, Burmese, Karen, Amharic, and Dari. In addition to the problem of finding interpreters for many of these languages, there have been problems with the Language Line interpretation service and with nonprofessional interpreters used for interpretation, according to comments made by the coordinator in our interview with her:

- It is not easy to get an interpreter right away (despite claims to the contrary made by Language Line).
- Even if the interpreter speaks the language, they may not know medical terminology.
- Some of the nonprofessional interpreters are refugees with limited English proficiency, insufficient to provide accurate interpretation.
- These interpreters may not know some concepts even in their first language.
- Sometimes counselors (trained social workers) serve as interpreters.

Services Provided at the Calgary Resettlement Centre

The Resettlement Assistance Program offers services to government-assisted refugees. Services include temporary accommodation in the CRC for up to 19 days, initial assessment, airport pickup, provision of clothes, and so on. During these 19 days, refugees get orientation on a daily basis for at least 2 hours a day on Canadian laws, weather, schools, domestic violence, and so on. They also get vaccinations, social security cards, Government Sales Tax (GST) credit, and intensive counseling and support for up to six weeks. After this initial support, they can access the Integrated Service Program for up to three years. These services include orientation, information on the resettlement process, counseling, referrals to other services, emergency translations, interpretation, house referrals, and social activities. Counselors help them look for an apartment, but the financial assistance they receive is insufficient for rent (only $700 a month for a family of five at the time of the study). The entire amount of assistance cannot exceed $1378 a month, which is the equivalent of what a Canadian citizen on welfare received from the government at the time of the study.

Based on the information we gathered from the Resettlement and Integration Services Coordinator, contextualized with the earlier research project we had conducted on the LINC program, our team (Ricento, postdoctoral fellow Andreea Cervatiuc, doctoral student Vladimir Pavlov) spent several months developing a research proposal that would enable us to gain insights into the lived experiences of a cohort of refugees that had spent time at the Resettlement House in Calgary and had moved into housing in the Calgary area. The project we developed was titled 'Linguistic and Cultural Barriers to Refugees' Access to Medical and Social Services' and ran from August 2009 through July 2011. The research was fully funded by the Research Chair I held at the Werklund School of Education, University of Calgary, which was supported by a local philanthropic organization and an anonymous donor. The purpose of the study was to gain a more sophisticated and comprehensive understanding of the sorts of challenges and barriers faced by refugees in their transition to living and working in Calgary, Canada. From an initial intake of 30 families in Phase I of the project, representing 120 people, we chose 6 focal families for Phase II, which involved monthly visits to their homes at which time structured and semi-structured interviews were conducted with family members (adults and children over 12 years of age if consented to by their parents) in one of 6 languages: Karen, Nepali, Somali, Dari, Spanish, or French. Native speakers of these languages provided real-time interpretation during which a research associate (Cervatiuc or Pavlov) was present; the associates also took notes, later digitalized, asked follow-up questions, and communicated with the interpreter and, at times, with the refugee informants through the interpreters, when necessary. The digitally recorded interviews were later transcribed in English. The countries of origin for the interviewees were Myanmar, Bhutan, Somalia, Afghanistan, Colombia, and Congo, respectively.

Over the course of nine months, we gained many insights into the obstacles faced by these individuals who had lived in Calgary anywhere from a few months to more than two years. We amassed over 100 hours of interviews with this remarkable group of people and came to learn about their immense courage and ability to persevere in the aftermath of unimaginable horrors and travails in their native countries, which included the witnessing of the murder and kidnapping of family members, and in several cases survival in relocation camps for up to 20 years. All of them expressed gratitude for having escaped the war, terrorism, political unrest, and lack of human rights that prevailed in their countries and that resulted in often harrowing journeys to staging countries before their arrival in Canada. Yet, the transition for the families into a normal life was, understandably, filled with anxiety, frustrations, and setbacks, despite the availability of support programs and community organizations that do their best to help this vulnerable population succeed.

Transitioning to Life in Calgary

The impact of border crossings on the lives of individuals, such as refugees, has many dimensions. One of the most significant findings from the Calgary project was the impact of dislocation from their native country on the ability of individuals to gain footing in a labor market that favors persons with Canadian work experience, which correlates with easier access to financial capital (e.g., a credit history which facilitates borrowing money to start a business), and with appropriate English language skills necessary for employment in occupations for which many were trained and credentialed in their countries of origin. The label 'refugee' itself is often a barrier to employment, and for foreign-born persons who are 'visible minorities' (an official term in Canada which generally means 'non-White'), the barrier to employment can be even higher.

To illustrate how individual refugees have experienced their transition to life in Canada, I will provide in-depth vignettes of a physician, his wife, and two children who fled from Colombia and landed in Canada as Government Assisted Refugees (GARS) identified through the United Nations High Commissioner for Refugees (UNHCR) (Chap. 4), and of a married couple from the Democratic Republic of the Congo (Chap. 5) whose histories in Canada reveal the perils faced by refugee claimants (persons who seek refugee status after arriving in Canada). Fernando,[3] a highly trained physician-specialist in neonatal surgery from Medellín, Colombia, faced numerous obstacles in his ultimately fruitless efforts to obtain licensure to practice his profession in Calgary; after persisting for several years in his struggle to have his credentials approved by the Provincial Medical Association, he found the best option available was to become a pharmacy technician, for which he had to complete a one-year program at a local college (Southern Alberta Institute of Technology), and he is now employed by a Drug Store chain in Calgary.[4] This was not the first or only example of the intransigence of the College of Physicians and Surgeons in Alberta when an applicant was from a country other than the United States, England, Australia, New Zealand, or South Africa; another physician from Colombia[5] that I interviewed in 2008 had been ignored by the licensing agency for five years until a physician colleague for whom he had served as a physician's assistant made a telephone call, and within 10 minutes this physician had been cleared to for a medical residency which led, eventually, to full licensure to practice medicine, after taking and passing three written exams and a laborious and protracted oral exam (personal interview with Dr. X, December 2008, Calgary).

The other two individuals whose stories will be related (Chap. 5) are a married couple from the Republic of the Congo. Patrick,[6] 47 years old, had a good life as a businessman in the informal economy of a low-income, African country until the onset of war and threats to his security required that he leave the country and come to Canada as a refugee claimant. Although Patrick had much less formal education than Fernando when he arrived in Montreal, his inability to borrow money from a bank necessary to buy a truck to become an independent businessman resulted in a severe diminution of his ability to use his skills and knowledge to participate in the Canadian economy. Patrick initially arrived in Montreal (Quebec) because of his fluency in French which he hoped would help him land a job and facilitate integration into Canadian society; he obtained a two-year engineering degree at a community college in Montreal, but even that credential (along with his native fluency in French) was not sufficient for him to find a job in the area for which his Canadian degree qualified him, so he moved to western Canada (Alberta) hoping that he would find a better future there. His 47-year-old wife, Chantal,[7] who was also a refugee claimant, and who had arrived in Canada after her husband had arrived, had not been able to obtain permanent resident status at the time of the interview after trying for more than ten years. The stress of not obtaining permanent resident status, which barred her from many social services, including full medical coverage, and prevented her from getting a job, led to serious mental anguish, resulting in a period of hospitalization. In the Congo, even poor people can enjoy a rich social support network, something that does not exist for Patrick or Chantal in Calgary.

Below, I provide some of the information on the cohort of refugees that our team interviewed in Phase I (Recruitment of Consultants), including ages, gender, country of origin, language in which they were interviewed (however, many of the people we interviewed spoke and were educated in other languages, sometimes up to five other languages, and these languages were recorded on the interview forms), and previous occupation(s). I have omitted the names of the individuals to preserve their anonymity. I also include the Recruitment Letter we used and the initial survey questionnaire we used in our initial interviews at the Calgary Resettlement Centre. The Recruitment Letter for Refugees was translated into all of the seven languages spoken by the refugees we interviewed at the Calgary Resettlement Centre; in addition, the Initial Survey Questionnaire (see below) was administered by persons with native competence in the language of the interviewee who translated each question (orally) and provided the respondents' answers (in English) on the form (the questionnaire was given only after the prospective interviewee had read the recruitment letter [in a language they understood] and signed and dated it. Any questions or concerns any of the participants had were responded to and all participants had the option to withdraw from the Phase II interviews at any time without penalty [details are provided in the Recruitment Letter for Refugees below]).

Recruitment Letter for Refugees

Dear Participant,

This letter invites you to participate in a research study we are conducting under the auspices of the English as an Additional Language (EAL) Chair, in the Faculty of Education, at the University of Calgary. The title of our study is ***Linguistic and Cultural Barriers to Refugees' Access to Medical and Social Services in Calgary***.

The purpose of this study is to investigate the issues related to linguistic and cultural barriers to refugees' access to medical and social services. We will seek to identify the relative effects of these impediments to refugees' integration into Canadian society, by following the lives of a cohort of refugee families as they transition from their 19-day orientation at the XXXXXX Resettlement Centre to living, working, and being educated in Calgary.

The project consists of two phases. For Phase I, we are looking for 50–60 refugees and for Phase II, we need 6 refugees and their families. If you decide to participate, your contribution will consist of the following:

Phase I:

- Sign a consent form.
- Complete a sociodemographic questionnaire (15–20 minutes).

Phase II:

- Sign a consent form.
- Allow the researcher(s) and a translator to visit you at home once a month, over a period of 12 months.
- Participate in structured and unstructured interviews (in your home) with the researcher(s), facilitated by a translator. Your spouse and your children who are 12 or older will participate in the interviews.

Participation in this research project is voluntary. You may choose not to participate or to withdraw from the study at any time without penalty. Upon withdrawal from the study, the data collected from you up to that point will be retained and used. Your participation or nonparticipation will not negatively impact any services you are currently receiving or your eligibility for future services from any agency involved in this research, nor will it benefit you in the refugee process. Your participation will in no way improve services received or otherwise positively impact the status of your refugee claim.

Those of you who participate in Phase II of the project will be paid $40 per family each time the researcher(s) and the translator visit you at home in order to interview you. We will refer to you or quote you in the study using either your real name or a coded name, based on your preference indicated in the consent form. The risks of participating in the study are no greater than those associated with your regular daily activities. The findings will be presented in a report, which will be posted on the EAL Chair website, in articles submitted for publication in refereed journals, and presentations at various conferences. An anonymous dataset may, in the future, be provided to other researchers who have gained the necessary ethics clearance.

If you have any questions, you can contact Dr. Thomas Ricento, (xxx) xxx–xxxx (e-mail address) or Dr. Andreea Cervatiuc, at (xxx) xxx–xxxx (e-mail address). Thank you in advance for your time and consideration. Your contribution is greatly appreciated.

Sincerely,

Dr. Thomas Ricento, Professor	Dr. Andreea Cervatiuc
English as an Additional Language Chair	Post-Doctoral Fellow
Faculty of Education	Faculty of Education
University of Calgary	University of Calgary
E-mail address	E-mail address
(xxx) xxx–xxxx	(xxx) xxx–xxxx

Initial Survey Questionnaire for Refugees at the Resettlement Center

The following survey is for the purpose of improving health care and social services for refugees in Canada. Participation in the survey is voluntary. This is part of a research project being conducted by Dr. Thomas Ricento and Dr. Andreea Cervatiuc of the University of Calgary.

Please circle or write the appropriate answer:

1. Gender: Male Female 2. Age: __________

3. a. How many people are in your family in Canada? ______

b. What are the ages and gender of your children in Canada?

1. __________________ 4. __________________

2. __________________ 5. __________________

3. __________________ 6. __________________

4. Highest Educational level attained:

Husband (H) Wife (W) Children (1, 2, 3, 4, 5, 6)

Lower than high school High school

College/University degree Post graduate/professional

degree

5. a. What is your current profession or occupation?

____

b. What was your profession or occupation before coming to Canada?

____

c. What occupation or profession do you plan to have in Canada?

____

d. What is your spouse's current profession or occupation?

____

e. What was your profession or occupation before coming to Canada?

____

f. What occupation or profession does your spouse plan to have in Canada?

____

6 . Native language: Husband: ___________ Wife: ____________________

Children: ____

____

7. a. What other languages do you speak or write?

____

b. Which of these languages do you use at home?

____

8. Describe your English language ability. ______________________________

____

9. Country of birth: ________________ Nationality: ______________

10. Spouse's country of birth: ___________ Nationality: ______________

11. Children's' country of birth: ______________________________

__________________ Nationalit(ies): ______________________

12. Mother's country of birth: ___________ Nationality: ______________

13. Father's country of birth: ___________ Nationality: ______________

14. Status in Canada:

Government Sponsored Refugee Refugee Claimant Other: ______________

15. a. Length of time in Canada: _____year(s) ______month(s)

b. Length of time in Calgary: _____years(s) _____month(s)

16. Would you be willing to participate in a research project over a period of one year, and for which you would be paid $480? We will provide detailed information on your role in this project if you are interested. There is no obligation to participate in this project after being given information about it.

17. How may we contact you if you want to learn more about the research project?

Telephone: ( ) _____________Cell Phone: ( ) ________________

Email: ____

18. Why did you leave your country?

____

____

19. What kind of problems did you face in your country?

____

Linguistic and Cultural Barriers to Refugees' Access to Medical and Social Services in Calgary

Phase I Demographic Summary

TOTAL NUMBER OF FAMILIES	30
TOTAL NUMBER OF PEOPLE PRESENT	46
TOTAL NUMBER OF PEOPLE REPRESENTED	120

	Language	*Number of families*	*Number of people present*	*Number of people represented*
1	Spanish	9	18	29
2	Karen	6	6	33
3	Nepali	5	10	30
4	French	4	4	13
5	Somali	4	4	5
6	Dari	1	2	7
7	Farsi	1	2	3

First Language Distribution by Number of Families

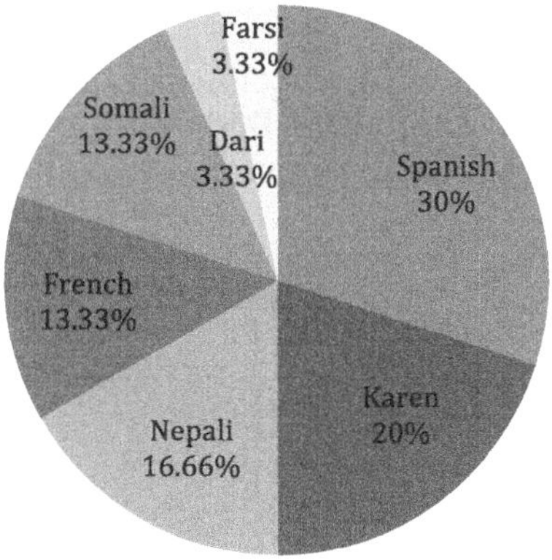

First Language Distribution by Number of People Present

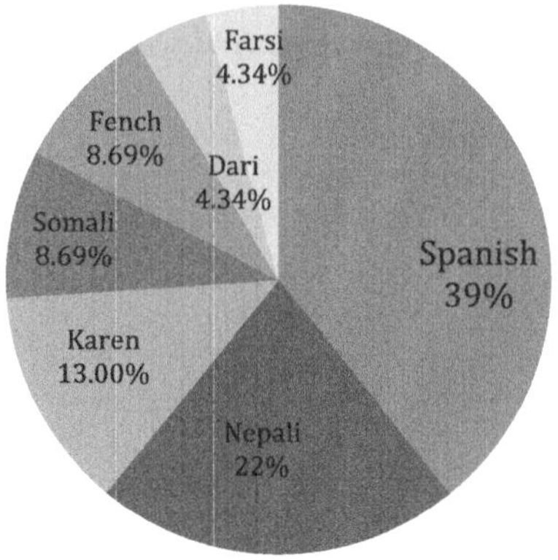

	Language	*Number of people present*
1	Spanish	18
2	Nepali	10
3	Karen	6
4	Somali	5
5	French	4
6	Dari	2
7	Farsi	2

First Language Distribution by Number of People Represented

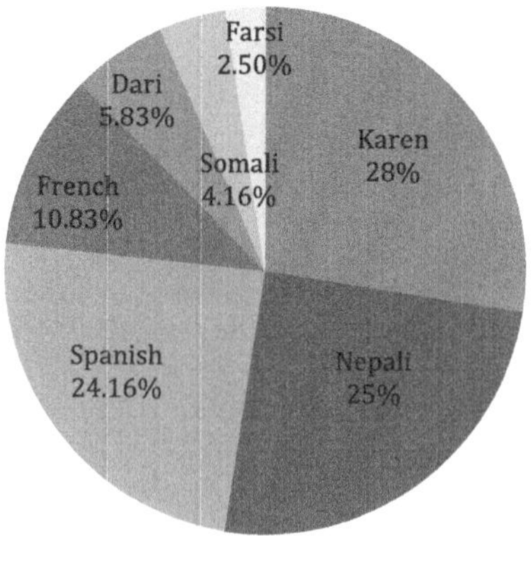

	Language	Number of people represented
1	Karen	33
2	Nepali	30
3	Spanish	29
4	French	13
5	Dari	7
6	Somali	5
7	Farsi	3

Linguistic and Cultural Barriers to Refugees' Access to Medical and Social Services in Calgary

Database of Phase I Participants

SUMMARY OF PHASE I DEMOGRAPHICS	
TOTAL NUMBER OF FAMILIES	**30**
TOTAL NUMBER OF PEOPLE PRESENT	**46**
TOTAL NUMBER OF PEOPLE REPRESENTED	**120**

1. FIRST LANGUAGE: SPANISH
COUNTRY: COLOMBIA
NUMBER OF FAMILIES: 9
NUMBER OF PEOPLE PRESENT: 18
NUMBER OF PEOPLE REPRESENTED: 29

	First language and country	Participant	Age	Civil status	Number of children in Canada	Children's ages	Number of people in the family in Canada	Previous occupation	Phone number
1	Spanish, Columbia	Male	51	Married	2	15, 9	4	Doctor (surgeon)	
2	Spanish, Colombia	Male	28	Married	0	N/A	2	Manager	
3	Spanish Colombia,	Male	47	Married	1	16	3	Carpenter	
4	Spanish, Colombia	Female	53	Married	3	28, 27, 25	5	Fashion designer	
5	Spanish, Colombia	Female	56	Married	0	N/A	2	QC supervisor	

(*continued*)

(continued)

	First language and country	Parti-cipant	Age	Civil status	Number of children in Canada	Children's ages	Number of people in the family in Canada	Previous occupation	Phone number
6	Spanish, Colombia	Female	37	Married	2	8, 4	2	Lawyer	
7	Spanish, Colombia	Female	41	Married	1	9	3	Social worker	
8	Spanish, Colombia	Female	42	Married	2	18, 13	4	Fashion designer	
9	Spanish, Colombia	Female	41	Married	2	16, 13	4	Psychologist	

2. FIRST LANGUAGE: KAREN COUNTRY: MYANMAR (BURMA) NUMBER OF FAMILIES: 6 NUMBER OF PEOPLE PRESENT: 6 NUMBER OF PEOPLE REPRESENTED: 33

	First language and country	Parti-cipant	Age	Civil status	Number of children in Canada	Children's ages	Number of people in the family in Canada	Previous occupation	Phone number
1	Karen, Myamar (Burma)	Male	35	Married	5	14, 12, 10, 6, 1	7	Boat taxi driver	
2	Karen, Myamar (Burma)	Male	39	Married	3	15, 13, 12	5	Bus driver	
3	Karen, Myamar (Burma)	Male	25	Married	1	4	3	Farmer	
4	Karen, Myamar (Burma)	Male	49	Married	7	18, 16, 16, 13, 10, 7, 3	9	Farmer	
5	Karen, Myamar (Burma)	Male	33	Married	3	12, 8, 4	5	Farmer	
6	Karen, Myamar (Burma)	Male	38	Married	4	16, 11, 9, 3	6	Farmer	

3. FIRST LANGUAGE: NEPALI
COUNTRY: BHUTAN
NUMBER OF FAMILIES: 5
NUMBER OF PEOPLE PRESENT: 10
NUMBER OF PEOPLE REPRESENTED: 30

	First language and country	*Parti-cipant*	*Age*	*Civil status*	*Number of children in Canada*	*Children's ages*	*Number of people in the family in Canada*	*Previous occupation*	*Phone number*
1	Nepali, Bhutan	Male	57	Married	4	33, 31, 29, 23	6	Farmer	
2	Nepali, Bhutan	Female	52	Married	4	27, 20, 15, 11	6	Salesperson	
3	Nepali, Bhutan	Male	42	Married	4	24, 20, 16, 12	6	Carpenter	
4	Nepali, Bhutan	Male	46	Married	5	23, 20, 18, 13, 4	7	Construction worker	
5	Nepali, Bhutan	Male	40	Married	2	15, 11	5	Construction worker	

4. FIRST LANGUAGE (for purposes of the interviews): FRENCH
COUNTRY: CONGO
NUMBER OF FAMILIES: 4
NUMBER OF PEOPLE PRESENT: 4
NUMBER OF PEOPLE REPRESENTED: 13

	First language and country	*Parti-cipant*	*Age*	*Civil status*	*Number of children in Canada*	*Children's ages*	*Number of people in the family in Canada*	*Previous occupation*	*Phone number*
1	French	Female	35	Married	4	7, 5, 4, 10 m.	6	Student	
2	French	Female	25	Married	1	6	2	Social worker	
3	French	Female	36	Single	2	11, 6	3	Salesperson	
4	French	Male	32	Single	1	1	2	Engineer	

5. FIRST LANGUAGE: DARI
COUNTRY: AFGHANISTAN
NUMBER OF FAMILIES: 1
NUMBER OF PEOPLE PRESENT: 2
NUMBER OF PEOPLE REPRESENTED: 7

	First language and country	*Participant*	*Age*	*Civil status*	*Number of children in Canada*	*Children's ages*	*Number of people in the family in Canada*	*Previous occupation*	*Phone number*
1	Dari, Afghanistan	Male	53	Married	5	23, 22, 19, 16, 14	7	Doctor	

6. FIRST LANGUAGE: SOMALI
COUNTRY: SOMALIA
NUMBER OF FAMILIES: 4
NUMBER OF PEOPLE PRESENT: 4
NUMBER OF PEOPLE REPRESENTED: 5

	First language and country	*Participant*	*Age*	*Civil status*	*Number of children in Canada*	*Children's ages*	*Number of people in the family in Canada*	*Previous occupation*	*Phone number*
1	Somali Somalia,	Female	24	Single	0	N/A	1	Salesperson	
2	Somali, Somalia	Female	57	Single	0	N/A	1	Taylor	
3	Somali, Somalia	Female	18	Single	0	N/A	1	Student	
4	Somali, Somalia	Male	50	Single	1	18	2	Teacher	

7. FIRST LANGUAGE: FARSI
COUNTRY: IRAN
NUMBER OF FAMILIES: 1
NUMBER OF PEOPLE PRESENT: 2
NUMBER OF PEOPLE REPRESENTED: 3

	First language and country	*Participant*	*Age*	*Civil status*	*Number of children in Canada*	*Children's ages*	*Number of people in the family in Canada*	*Previous occupation*	*Phone number*
1	Farsi	Female	29	Married	1	7 m.	3	Dental assistant	

In choosing the families from the group that had volunteered to participate in Phase II of our study, we sought to have a reasonably representative sample of people from the total of 120 individuals who were represented in the initial survey we administered at the Calgary Resettlement Centre (Phase I interview). We took into account factors such as family size, gender, age, marital status, regional balance, educational attainment, length of time in Canada, previous employment, current employment in Canada, diversity of languages, and availability of consultants to participate in Phase II of the study. In the end, members of the six families that participated in Phase II interviews reflected a good balance in terms of the factors described above. All of the individuals (listed below) from the six focal families participated in most or all of the Phase II interviews and were willing to spend anywhere from one hour to two or more hours per session each month with our research team in their homes. They were gracious and happy to share their experiences and insights with our team members throughout the project.

The monthly interviews that we conducted in the homes of our consultants followed sequenced scripted questions, with opportunities for follow-ups and extended discussions in many cases. The original intake survey questionnaire (provided earlier) provided us with useful details on many aspects of the refugees, including information on the family members, the languages they spoke (first, second, etc.), educational attainment, the countries they had lived in prior to arriving in Canada, their professions prior to arriving in Canada, and their legal status in Canada. After the recorded interviews in Phase II had been translated and transcribed into English by our six translators, postdoctoral fellow Andreea Cervatiuc and doctoral student Vladimir Pavlov, using a grounded theory approach, identified potential emergent themes in the transcribed interviews; after cross-checking with our refugee consultants and interpreters for purposes of clarification of words, phrases, and/or ideas that had been transcribed, the transcriptions were accordingly revised, and from those revised transcriptions, thematic clusters were proposed, subject to further revision. This was a painstaking process that required many months of analysis and cross-checking between Cervatiuc, Pavlov, Ricento, the interpreters, and interviewees to ensure a high degree of confidence in inter-rater reliability across the research team.

The purpose of the questions asked in Interview 1 of Phase II of the study was to obtain baseline information on the refugees (including of family members who were not present for the initial interview). Based on the questions we posed to our consultants, the team identified two thematic clusters for Interview 1: (1) Identity and Immigration Story, and (2) Living Conditions, Access to Medical, Educational, Social, and Legal Services, Employment/Income Situation, Housing Conditions, and Social Life Prior to Coming to Canada. Within these two macro clusters, 11 topics were identified and within each of these topics, subthemes were identified and exemplified with supporting quotations from the interviews. In Interview 2, two thematic clusters were identified: (1) Integration and Adjustment to Life in Canada, and (2) Living Conditions, Access to Medical, Educational, Social, and Legal Services, Employment/Income Situation, Housing Conditions, and Social Life Prior to Coming to Canada. Within these two macro clusters, ten topics were identified and subthemes were exemplified with supporting quotations from the interviews. In Interviews 3, 4, 5, and 6 two thematic clusters were identified: (1) Challenges, Hardships, and Frustrations in the Past Month, and (2) Living Conditions, Access to Medical, Educational, Social, and Legal Services, Employment/Income Situation, Housing Conditions, and Social Life in the Past Month. Within these two thematic clusters, 12 topics were identified and subthemes were exemplified with quotations from the interviews. Below are the topics and subthemes that were identified based on analysis of the transcriptions of the interviews conducted in the homes of the refugees in Phase II of the project.

Phase II Interview Questions

1. Interview 1: (Baseline questions)
   - Family they have in Canada
   - Reasons for coming to Canada
   - Journey to Canada
   - Expectations about life in Canada
   - The degree to which their expectations about life in Canada were met
   - Unexpected things about life in Canada
   - Biggest challenges and difficulties in the countries where they lived before
   - Current immigration status
   - Living conditions in the country/countries where they lived prior to immigrating to Canada
   - Quality of health care in the country/countries where they lived prior to immigrating to Canada
   - Quality of children's schooling in the country/countries where they lived prior to immigrating to Canada
2. Interview 2: (Adjustment to life in Canada)
   - Adjustment to life in Canada
   - Positive aspects about life in Canada
   - Negative aspects about life in Canada
   - Comparison between life in Canada and life in their home country
   - Biggest challenges and hardships in Canada
   - Biggest sources of support
   - Living conditions in Canada
   - Level of satisfaction with medical services and health care in Canada
   - Level of satisfaction with children's schooling in Canada
   - Level of satisfaction with the services received from social workers and government agencies
3. Interviews 3, 4, 5, 6: (Ongoing issues and changes from the previous month(s))
   - Biggest challenges in the past month
   - Biggest sources of support in the past month
   - Level of satisfaction with their life in Calgary in the past month

- Things that were particularly frustrating living in Calgary in the past month
- Progress in terms of integrating into life in Calgary in the past month
- Changes in their living conditions in the past month
- Types of medical appointments in the past month
- The level of satisfaction with the medical services received
- Manner of communication
- Visits to children's school in the past month
- Level of satisfaction with the school visit
- Manner of communication

The table below contains information on the participants in Phase II of the study.

List of Participants' Pseudonyms

Colombian Participants

Pseudonym	*Real name*	*Age*	*Gender*	*Family member*	*Current occupation in Canada*	*Occupation in the country of origin*
Fernando, a 51-year-old male Colombian refugee		51	Male	Husband	EAP student at Mount Royal University	Physician
Maria, a 44-old-female Colombian refugee		44	Female	Wife	ESL student	Accountant
Jose, a 17-year-old male Colombian refugee		17	Male	Son	High school student	Student

Congolese Participants

Pseudonym	*Real name*	*Age*	*Gender*	*Type of family member*	*Current occupation in Canada*	*Occupation in the country of origin*
Patrick, a 47-year-old male Congolese refugee		47	Male	Husband	ESL student	Salesperson
Chantal, a 37-year-old male Congolese refugee		37	Female	Wife	Unemployed	Student

Burmese Participants

Pseudonym	*Real name*	*Age*	*Gender*	*Type of family member*	*Occupation in the country of origin*	*Occupation in the country of origin*
Co, a 51-year old male Burmese refugee		51	Male	Husband	Unemployed	Farmer
Mya, a 45-year-old female Burmese refugee		45	Female	Wife	ESL student	Housewife
Sandi, a 20-year old-female Burmese refugee		20	Female	Daughter	Student	Student
Arun, an 18-year old-male Burmese refugee		18	Male	Son	Student	Student
Maung, an 18-year old-male Burmese refugee		18	Male	Son	Student	Student
Lwin, a 15-year-old male Burmese refugee		15	Female	Daughter	Student	Student

Somali Participants

Pseudonym	*Real name*	*Age*	*Gender*	*Family member*	*Current occupation in Canada*	*Occupation in the country of origin*
Aziza, a 58-year old-female Somali refugee		58	Female	Mother	Unemployed	Taylor/ cleaner/store owner
Ayanna, a female Somali refugee		20	Female	Daughter		
Abdi, a male Somali refugee		16	Male	Son		
Dalamar, a male Somali refugee		15				

Bhutanese Refugees

Pseudonym	*Real name*	*Age*	*Gender*	*Family member*	*Current occupation in Canada*	*Occupation in the country of origin*
Bikash, a 59-year-old male Bhutanese refugee		59	Male	Husband		Farmer
Sreya, a 55-year-old female Bhutanese refugee		55	Female	Wife		Housewife
Bishwa, a male Bhutanese refugee			Male	Son		
Pranish, a male Bhutanese refugee			Male	Son		
Ashis			Male	Son		

Afghani -1 Refugees

Pseudonym	*Real name*	*Age*	*Gender*	*Family member*	*Current occupation in Canada*	*Occupation in the country of origin*
Babur, a 55-year-old male Afghani refugee		55	Male	Husband		Physician
Ava, a 46-year-old female Afghani refugee		46	Female	Wife		Teacher
Badria, an 18-year-old female Afghani refugee		18	Female	Daughter		
Asal, a 16-year-old female Afghani refugee		16	Female	Daughter		

Afghani -2 Refugees

Pseudonym	*Real name*	*Age*	*Gender*	*Family member*	*Current occupation in Canada*	*Occupation in the country of origin*
Atash, a 42-year-old male Afghani refugee		42	Male	Husband		Manager
Awrang, a 36-year-old female Afghani refugee		36	Female	Wife		Teacher

Notes

1. See Chap. 6 for an extended discussion on this point.
2. A refugee claimant (Chantal) had been waiting more than ten years for a decision at the time we interviewed her in 2010. Although her husband Patrick had already obtained his Canadian permanent resident status in 2001, her application was delayed for reasons that were unknown to both Chantal and Patrick. Their situation is discussed in more detail in Chap. 5 in this book.

3. A pseudonym.
4. The program at Southern Alberta Institute of Technology (SAIT) consists of one semester of courses and a second semester of Practicum. According to information on the SAIT website for this program (accessed August 23, 2020), the current median salary for pharmacy technician is $28,200 (Canadian Dollars) per year, a salary far below the average income of a practicing licensed physician in Alberta, which was $354,492 (Canadian Dollars) in 2019, $28,200 being a mere 8% of what Fernando could have earned in Alberta as a physician; as a neonatal surgeon with 20 years clinical experience, it is likely he would have earned much more than the average income for physicians in Alberta.
5. I am unable to provide the identity of this person because he requested that I not use his name or affiliation due to fears that his family in Colombia would be at risk.
6. A pseudonym.
7. A pseudonym.

References

Abu-Laban, B., Derwing, T., Krahn, H., Mulder, M., & Wilkinson. (1999) *The Settlement Experiences of Refugees in Alberta*. Prairie Centre of Excellence for Research on Immigration and Integration and Population Research Laboratory. Downloaded on March 13, 2009, from http://pcerii.metropolis.net/Virtual%20Library/RefugeeStudy/.

Balley, B. & Builthuis, M. (2004). The Changing Portrait of Homelessness. Our Diverse Cities 1, 119–123. Download on March 16, 2009, from: http://canada.metropolis.net/researchpolicy/cities/publication/diverse_cite_magazine_e.pdf.

Fantino, A. M., & Colak, A., (2001). Refugee Children in Canada: Searching for Identity. *Child Welfare* 80 (5), 587–596.

Martin, F., & Curran, J. (2007). Separated Children: A Comparison of the Treatment of Separated Child Refugees Entering Australia and Canada. *International Journal of Refugee Law* 19(4), 440–470.

Pruebber, V. J. & Tanasescu, A. (2007). Housing Issues of Immigrants and Refugees in Canada. Downloaded on March 14, 2009, from http://www.calgary.ca/docgallery/bu/cns/homelessness/housing_issues_immigrants_refugees.pdf

Ricento, T., Cervatiuc, A., MacMillan, F., & Massoudi, S. (2008). Insights into Funded ESL Programs. Report on the LINC Program. Calgary: University of Calgary.

Saulnier, C. (2008). Refugee women seeking to stay in Canada treated badly. *CCPA Monitor* 15 (5), 27.

Schellenberg, G. & Maheux, H. (2007). Immigrants' perspectives on their first four years in Canada: Highlights from three waves of the Longitudinal Survey of Immigrants to Canada. Statistics Canada. Downloaded on March 16, 2009, from: http://www.statcan.gc.ca/bsolc/olc-cel/olc-cel?lang=eng&catno=11-008-X20070009627.

Stewart, J. L. (2008). *Children affected by war: A bio-ecological investigation into their psychosocial and educational needs.* Doctoral dissertation. University of Manitoba.

CHAPTER 4

The Martinez Family

Abstract In this chapter, I provide a detailed narrative on the lives of the Martinez family as they transitioned to life in Canada over a nine-month period after fleeing Colombia. Fernando is a pediatric surgeon, his wife is an accountant, and their two children are in middle school and high school. In this chapter, I use the exact words of family members who tell us about their experiences on a range of issues in great detail, including frustrations in gaining employment and licensure (for Fernando), dealing with various types of discrimination (in the workplace, in the classroom, with school policies), and with their experiences in ESL classes. The interviews were conducted in Spanish and later transcribed into English.

Keywords Martinez family profiles • Colombia • International Medical Graduate • ESL programs • Canadian professional societies • Medical licensure • Erasure of identity • Social capital

Of the profiles of refugees documented in this book, I found the story of Fernando Martinez,[1] his wife, and two children to be one of the most compelling and one that I can most easily relate to on a personal level. For one thing, I have firsthand knowledge of their country, Colombia, having been a Fulbright Professor there in the summer of 1989 during which time I gave lectures and workshops at four universities and four Colombo-Americanos, and visited many cities and regions of the country. My visit

T. Ricento, *Refugees in Canada*,
https://doi.org/10.1007/978-3-030-76453-1_4

coincided with a period of great violence throughout the country in which armed far-right paramilitary groups, often working in coordination with crime syndicates, were engaged in low-intensity conflict with a number of left-wing guerrilla groups; this multifaceted intra-country conflict began around 1964 with devastating results for the people of Colombia; according to a study by Colombia's National Centre for Historical Memory (2013), 220,000 people have died in the conflict between 1958 and 2013, most of them civilians (177,307 civilians and 40,787 fighters) and more than five million civilians were forced from their homes between 1985 and 2012, generating the world's second largest population of internally displaced persons. The Martinez family were among the millions of victims of that violence who fled Colombia, many of whom landed in the United States and Canada as government-sponsored refugees.

When I first met Fernando Martinez in downtown Calgary, after the interviews had been completed, I felt an instant connection. We spoke mostly in Spanish, which of course influenced and enhanced our communication. I found Fernando to be very personable, outgoing, and quite willing to share his views on many issues; in fact, his willingness to share his experiences in great detail and provide critical insights about what he and his family had experienced since arriving in Calgary rendered him as somewhat of an outlier compared to most of the other refugees we interviewed. It must be kept in mind that all of the families we interviewed in Phase II of the project were grateful to have landed in Canada, either as government-assisted Refugees or as asylum seekers (refugee claimants), under the protection and with the financial support of the Canadian government, and were mindful of the benefits they had enjoyed as noncitizens in a foreign country, having escaped often life-threatening situations in another country. It is completely understandable that persons in such a situation would not want to directly criticize any aspects of their Canadian experiences. It is certainly the case that the three members of the Martinez family that we interviewed were grateful for having landed in a country where they didn't have to worry about their personal safety and where the government provided financial assistance, free health care, high quality education for their children, and a promising future. The principal factor that animated the narrative of Fernando and Maria Martinez was the fact that their material situation in Colombia was relatively privileged and the barriers to resume their careers and accustomed lifestyles in Canada seemed to be insurmountable. The gap between expectations and experiences of the six focal families in this study varied considerably, as did their reactions and responses to challenges posed by their refugee status, especially with regard to re-establishing their careers and gaining financial security. Differences in educational attainment, profession in the home country, family size, language proficiency in English, ability to cope with Canadian climate, culture, customs, and bureaucracy were important factors in how each family member viewed their particular situation and how they viewed their future prospects. While there were commonalities in their experiences, there is no doubt that individual differences, along with the factors mentioned above, played an important role in the integration process of each individual. While the narratives that will be related in this and the following chapter provide insights into how individuals dealt with myriad challenges in their long journeys that led them to Calgary, it must be remembered that it is dangerous to make generalizations based solely, or primarily, on their country of origin, ethnicity, linguistic repertoire, educational level, or any other 'categorical' descriptor that can be used to 'explain' let along 'justify' why some groups/peoples are more successful than others integrating into 'Canadian' society, such as that society is perceived and constructed by narratives of what is 'normal' and 'expected' behavior; however, it should also be kept in mind that Canada is a White settler immigrant-receiving country of roughly 38 million people founded (it is claimed in Canadian historical documents) by the 'French' and the 'English' ('races'), but whose first inhabitants had arrived centuries prior to the arrival of the first European settlers.

Background on the Martinez Family Prior to Arriving in Canada

Fernando is a pediatric surgeon who had his own clinic in Colombia and had worked in four other clinics in the city of Medellín. His wife, Maria, is a certified accountant and had her own business, doing assessments for various companies. The Martinez family had an excellent lifestyle in Colombia; they had high salaries and lived in a spacious and modern apartment in which each bedroom had its own bathroom. They hired two housekeepers to help them with various chores (not uncommon for middle-class families in many countries in Central and South America) and they also owned a small farm in the countryside (also not uncommon in many countries in the region). They went on many vacations and were able to send their children to private schools where they were provided an

English immersion curriculum, which proved invaluable for their future lives in Canada. Maria commented that she believes that due to the excellent education that their son Jose received in Colombia, he is three grades ahead of his classmates in Canada.

The events that led to the Martinez family attaining government-assisted refugee status and their eventual move to Canada from Medellín, Colombia, are rather horrific. One of Fernando's brothers was kidnapped by a guerilla group who sequestered him for about six months; Fernando had to negotiate with the guerillas and ended up paying a lot of money to secure his brother's release. His sister-in-law had also been kidnapped previously. Fernando finally made an arrangement with the guerillas that, by paying a monthly fee, no one from his family would be kidnapped or injured. Finally, the family was living in such constant fear that the guerillas would kidnap and threaten to kill other family members, and escalate their demands for more money, they decided to apply for refugee status. This was not an easy decision because leaving Colombia meant leaving their home, their professions, their friends and family,[2] and their language (Spanish) for uncharted waters. Once their application for refugee status was approved, they had less than one week to prepare properly for their trip, which included dealing with their professional commitments, family relations, and saying goodbye—possibly forever—to Colombia—their country—and the only life they had ever known.

The Martinez family had been living in Calgary for about three years at the time the research project began. At the time of our interviews, Fernando was 51 years old, his wife was 44 years old, their son Jose was 17 years old, and their daughter was 11 years old. The financial support the family received from the government was initially C$1100 a month; however, after one year, effective September 2010, the amount was reduced to $924 per month. According to Fernando (September 30, 2010), "the government agencies try to push people to do survival jobs, which means: cleaning. Even that type of job is difficult to obtain. I have applied sometimes for cleaning jobs and my applications have been rejected because the employers considered me overqualified for this type of job." He had been told by an advisor to prepare a resume without mentioning his career experience; the advisor said that Fernando should say that he finished high school only, otherwise he would never be able to get a survival job (September 2010). Despite the drastic drop in social and economic status, and the loss of access to the lifestyle he and his family enjoyed in Colombia, Fernando and his wife at least did not have to worry about their personal safety or that of their children. In a word, they were grateful to be living away from the terrors at home; however, as will be revealed in the discussion that follows, there were times when Fernando considered returning to Colombia, even at the risk of losing his life, rather than continue living a life that essentially required that he renounce his identity as a physician, and as a man who had lost nearly all of his self-respect as a highly trained professional and head of a household, respected by society and peers, because of circumstances completely out of his control. Fortunately, two of Fernando's brothers and his mother, who were already living in Calgary, got together regularly to celebrate birthdays, holidays, and maintain a semblance of normal family life; Fernando visits one of his brothers on Sundays and sometimes his mother comes to his apartment and they have a family night and watch a movie. This certainly provides solace and comfort for Fernando and his family since lack of money and limitations with English make it difficult to have contact with friends or people outside their family.

Soon after arriving in Calgary, Fernando sent his Medical Diplomas to Ottawa for an evaluation. Although the Medical Board finally accepted them for review, he is still waiting for a response. He also contacted the College of Physicians and Surgeons of Alberta and has received no support from them, other than being told that 'we have enough physicians in Alberta,' an assertion that is refuted by reliable data. He was also told that what he needed to work on more than anything else was his spoken English; he was told that if he had the opportunity to work as an assistant to a physician, he would be able to learn the medical terms and protocols in six to ten months, and after that he would be able to perform surgeries because of his many years of experience (advice which turned out to be incorrect). In the meantime, he has been networking and talking to people in the medical field in Calgary to gain information about the licensure process. He was told that it might take him four to five years to get licensure, if he is lucky; however, since he already has two specialties from Colombia, he felt it would be a waste of time to learn a third specialty, for example, in internal medicine or in family medicine. He also found out that many immigrant physicians pass all the exams and are still not accepted for residencies.[3] There is a limited number of surgeons in Calgary who perform specific surgeries that Fernando used to perform in Colombia (on newborn and prematurely born infants), yet the intellectual and professional capital that Fernando possesses is simply not recognized by gatekeepers who have their own agenda and reasons (mostly economic) for restricting access by International Medical Graduates (IMGs) to the practice of medicine in the province (Bauder 2003).

Fernando summed up his feelings in this way:

> *It is extremely difficult, almost impossible, to get immersed in the medical field in this country. It is so difficult that sometimes I think that I am in a different planet. The medical system in this country is too discriminatory and elitist. In my country the medical system is so different, it is more open ... here it seems to be a very 'tightly closed circle.' It doesn't matter if I approach them and tell them that I am a qualified professional in the medical field and that I have twenty years' experience as a Pediatric Surgeon; that means 'zero.'* (August 28, 2010)

A month later, when asked by the research project interviewer 'What do you find negative about your life in Canada?' Fernando answered:

> *What I find negative of my life in Canada is the language barrier ... In order to get recognition of my certificates as a Medical Surgeon, I am asked to fulfill so many difficult requirements. It is easier to win the lotto than to be accepted as a professional in Canada.* (September 30, 2010)

The loss of Fernando's professional status, compounded by the English language barrier, effectively erased most of the hard-earned social and cultural capital he brought to Canada; faced with nearly insurmountable obstacles, Fernando sought alternative solutions to survive in Canada, including opening a restaurant/bar; in the meantime, he and his wife took general English classes at a local Language Instruction for Newcomers to Canada (LINC) program and after that, specialized English courses at a local college, while hoping against hope that one day Fernando would be able to work in the medical field. Fernando did not passively accept his circumstances; he complained about the content and pedagogy in his LINC classes (and he found most of the courses he was enrolled in to be unhelpful in attaining the skills he would need to practice his profession in Canada[4]); he expressed his views on how he was ignored by the medical staff at a local hospital when he brought his daughter there for an illness that he had correctly diagnosed; in short, he confidently gave voice during the interviews (in Spanish) about what he found unacceptable in how he was received in the language classroom, by the medical establishment, and how the requirements to obtain work in Calgary required 'Canadian experience,' a Catch-22 requirement that rendered him and other similarly situated refugees unemployable for all but the lowest paying jobs.

The Loss of Social Capital

In the first interview session with Fernando, Maria, and their son, Jose, six scripted questions were asked that focused primarily on the background of family members, their lives in their home country prior to coming to Canada, and the factors that led to their arrival in Canada as refugees. In discussing their lives in Colombia, Fernando, Maria, and Jose offered observations that, directly or indirectly, highlight what is lost when one leaves a world where one's identity, and one's thoughts and desires can be expressed and shared and enters another world where even one's most basic needs are difficult to articulate in the local language (English, in this case). It is not just that Fernando cannot work as a physician or that his wife isn't able to continue in her career as an accountant, or that their son cannot demonstrate his academic achievement and knowledge in Calgary schools in the way that it was recognized, praised, and valued in Colombia that creates a sense of frustration and exasperation; rather, the costs and limitations of not having a mastery of language or deep knowledge of and facility with local customs and norms have had a significant negative impact on their emotions and self-worth as human beings. Here are some examples to illustrate the costs of leaving one's language and culture behind; these responses were in answer to question 3: 'Can you tell us the story of how you came to Canada as a refugee? How hard was it? Were there any sacrifices that you needed to make to come here?':

Maria commented on her loss of social status:

Maria: *I was a Certified Accountant (in Colombia). I had my own business. I used to assess several companies. I was doing financially well. But here, I can just study English because without a good level of English it is not possible to have access to do something different than a 'survival job.' We had a high quality of life in Colombia. I was recognized by people as 'the wife of Dr. Fernando Martinez.' But here, Dr. Fernando Martinez is not the 'Dr. Martinez'; he is just Fernando, and logically, I am only 'one more person.'*

Jose: *Remember how you sacrificed leaving your family.*

Maria: *Yes, that was the greatest sacrifice … leaving behind my family. That affected me so much!* (August 28, 2010)

Everyone spoke about the ease of doing things in Medellín, Colombia, and how difficult most aspects of living in Calgary had become:

Jose: *In my country, I didn't need to work to receive so many benefits from the good conditions of living. Moreover, I had support from all the family in Colombia; I really liked living in that social and financial condition.*

Fernando: *In Medellín, Colombia, it is so easy to go from one place to another. If you need something, it is so easy to obtain it … The relationship with neighbors or other people is different in Colombia. If I was in need of childcare to go out to do something urgent, any neighbor or friend will do it for me. There are no limitations to obtain childcare. It is so difficult to be out of our environment. Being away from our social, financial, and familiar life is so hard. The major difficulty for us is the lack of language. It is the greatest difficulty, not being able to explain our needs, our thoughts, or our abilities to do something. We feel discriminated and underestimated for not speaking good English. I feel confident that if I am compared to other surgeons, there is a lot of knowledge and experience that they could acquire from me.* (August 28, 2010)

Jose's comment refers to the fact that he had to take a part-time job at KFC (Kentucky Fried Chicken), working four to eight hours a week, with a minimum shift of four hours and the maximum shift of eight hours in order to cover some of his personal expenses, something he didn't have to do in Colombia. Also, Fernando mentioned in the interview of December 9, 2010, that

> *He (Jose) complains that sometimes he feels frustrated because he has a supervisor from the Philippines who mistreats the staff. He has never been mistreated, not even at home. That is a situation he is suffering for being an immigrant. It was very different from all the information we received in Colombia about life in Canada. If I would have imagined even 5% of this reality, I would rather take the risk of being killed over there than coming to live in all this situation in this country. It is a very difficult change we have had.*

Fernando is aware that he has left a relatively privileged life behind in Colombia compared to others who had a bad situation in Colombia and for whom coming to Canada changed their life for the better:

> *For example, I have some relatives who had a bad financial situation and quality of life in Colombia. Coming to Canada changed their life completely for good. The quality of life they have here is very good for them. On the contrary, for us it is bad based on the privileges we had over there. As I mentioned before, if any of my children got sick they were seen with priority by my colleagues. Here it is the opposite; my daughter has been sick for two weeks now and the doctor didn't prescribe anything. Even though I know what her problem is, I cannot do anything because I cannot get the right drugs for her without a prescription. That makes the situation more difficult.* (December 9, 2010)

Professional courtesy for family members in the medical profession has also been customary in North America for a long time; yet, such courtesy is unavailable to Fernando, another reminder of his diminished status as a highly trained, but *foreign* trained, refugee physician.

Travails with English

Beginning with the first interview with the Martinez family on August 28, 2010, language was mentioned as an important factor for nearly all aspects of life in Calgary for members of the Martinez family. In what follows, I will present the various ways that Fernando, Maria, and Jose have characterized their experiences with English language learning and use, including their views on the ways in which it is taught in various programs, along with the changes in curriculum and teaching philosophy that they believe could enhance their learning experience. They offered frank, often critically incisive, analyses of the English classes they were enrolled in, and in the case of Jose, how perceptions of his 'foreignness' in high school, in some cases, resulted in negative evaluations of his intellectual and academic abilities. Fernando and Maria talk about the language requirements for gaining employment in their fields—medicine and accounting —and express frustration in the mismatch between the curricula and pedagogical approaches in their ESL classes and what they need to succeed professionally in Canada. Jose spoke about his frustration with the slow pace of his classes and the culture of the classroom, specifically reflected in how teachers and students interact, and how those interactions are considerably different from those he experienced in Colombia. Their views should be of interest to language teachers in similar adult ESL/EAL programs, and to all teachers who have recent immigrant students in their classrooms in Canada.

Learning English Is More Than Learning English

Teachers in adult second language programs often believe that their job is to provide their students with the 'instruments of communication' in order to help them survive and eventually integrate into the local (target) society. As someone who taught adult ESL/EFL classes in a variety of programs in California, Massachusetts, Japan, and elsewhere, I became familiar with curricula that often focused on grammar, pronunciation, and vocabulary associated with particular 'functions' that often related to some aspect of 'American culture,' an elusive, subjective construct, at best, and often viewed and taught prescriptively by textbook writers and curriculum planners. In California, in the 1980s, I was an instructor in a community college adult noncredit ESL program; at the time, the goal of courses was to teach 'competencies' such as reading prescription drug instructions, how to use the local transportation system, read and understand advertisements in newspapers for housing rentals, and similar topics. The dropout rate in many of these courses at the college was often very high, even though the courses were free and the instructors friendly, helpful, and dedicated. In fact, I found that the greatest benefit for the course that I taught at this particular community college was that it provided an opportunity for people from different backgrounds to socialize and discuss things that were actually happening in their lives, that is, about 'reality' outside the classroom and human relations and interactions within the classroom. What I remembered more than anything else about that class was that a sense of community within the classroom, however that might be fostered, was far more valuable than any particular grammar or vocabulary that was learned. Relationships developed in the classroom setting, and sometimes extended beyond the classroom, brought people back week after week, I think, because there was a sense of connection and community between people very different from each other in terms of culture, language, economic, and social status, and with very different short-term and often long-term goals and interests. The curriculum was limited in what it could possibly achieve in 5 classroom hours per week for 13 weeks; however, students experienced those hours, not just as language learners but as individuals seeking to make human connections with others in the class, and those experiences likely had an impact on how they felt about themselves in their new environment in the United States, and whether that feeling could motivate, or demotivate, their ongoing learning of English, moving toward a positive engagement, perhaps even integration, within the local community (see Norton 2000 on the concept of 'investment' in second language learning).

The research for which I was the P.I. in a local LINC program in Calgary in 2007–2008 provided insights into the curriculum, program goals, and teaching philosophy of teachers that, in some sense, validate the intuitions I have just expressed about the 'hidden' benefits that may be overlooked and underrated with regard to adult ESL learning. Although we found the teachers in the LINC program to be motivated and well-intentioned, they were nonetheless guided by what we identified to be a *transactional* curriculum meta-orientation in their approach to pedagogy (Cervatiuc and Ricento 2012). The comments made by Fernando and Maria about their experiences in various ESL classes further validate our conclusions from that earlier study of the LINC program, although the site of the 2007–2008 LINC project is different from the LINC site where Fernando and Maria attended classes. In our conversations with the Martinez family, we heard stories of classroom events that created a sense of frustration at not being 'heard' by others they interacted with (including their teachers) as fully formed adult human beings, as people with knowledge and a desire to share that knowledge in a classroom setting.

Fernando expressed the view on more than one occasion that the classes he had taken in the LINC program were not appropriate for his needs and he felt much of it was a waste of time. In various interviews, he provided quite specific comments about the English language instruction that was provided in the local LINC program, and also in an EAP (English for Academic Purposes) course at a local community college. For example, he noted that the different needs, ages, and backgrounds of students should be taken into account in the development of courses and curricula:

> *For example, it is not the same to teach English to my mother, who is a senior of 78 years, as it is to teach to my children or myself, who have completely different ages, interests, and backgrounds.* (September 30, 2010)

Fernando noted that he already had some reading skills in English that he developed in Colombia in order to read medical articles connected to his profession. Although he had made some progress in developing skills in listening, writing, and speaking in his LINC classes at the time of our interviews, he found that the lack of opportunity to interact with English-speaking Canadians had limited his listening ability:

> *I would like to have more interaction with English-speaking Canadians. I was an instructor in my home country and learned to set up straightforward objectives and evaluate my students to measure my achievements in teaching ... The opportunities given to students to interact to practice English are very limited. The distribution of the students in the classroom is uneven. I was in a classroom with many youngsters who have different interests and I was asked to have conversation with them which was boring for both. For example, we were given the topic of abortion to discuss. This topic was completely of no interest for a youth. Every time that we were asked to discuss any topic I noticed the unpleasant expression on his face and I felt the same way. I consider that a waste of time.* (September 30, 2010)

Another aspect of Fernando's frustration with language concerns his inability to express his thoughts and emotions in English, even though he is now able to understand more and communicate with English speakers[5]:

> *Emotions are the most difficult thing to express in English. Now that I am taking my courses in medical communication, I have difficulty expressing to patients that I am interested in their issues and that I care much for them and I need to know more about their emotions related to the problem, to be able to help more.* (September 30, 2010)

Another criticism voiced by Fernando concerned the English language input he was exposed to in his class in the LINC program. He found that communicating in class with other immigrants with their different accents does not help him develop competence in communicating with native English speakers:

> *When I communicate with immigrants (for example Russian, Chinese, etc.), who have different accents, it doesn't help me much. I realized that it is easy for Canadians to understand immigrants when speaking English because they have the roots of the language, but for me it is difficult to understand speakers from different languages.* (September 30, 2010)

Teachers and researchers may come to different conclusions about the benefits of exposure to accented 'non-native' English input in heterogeneous second language learning classrooms in English-dominant countries; however, the view of learners on this matter certainly cannot be dismissed out of hand by 'experts' any more than we 'experts' should dismiss complaints about inappropriate or ineffective teaching methods or curricular content expressed by language learners.

Fernando's Experiences in an English for Academic Purposes Course

After completing his course at the LINC program, Fernando enrolled in a course at a local college in Calgary: EAP1, English for Academic Purposes. The main purpose of the course is to learn to write essays; Fernando found that the course had very little relevance for his professional development as a physician or for someone in the health profession:

> *Practicing writing does not fulfill my career purposes. It would be of more benefit for me to practice listening and speaking. Unfortunately, those areas are not practiced enough in this course. In my case, writing is a secondary need. We practice listening every three weeks for half an hour only and we use some topics that are ridiculous to us. Other than that, we practice mostly writing with the disadvantage of not using a dictionary. In some cases, we might use a paper dictionary, but not an electronic one. I asked the instructor to show me any article confirming that the use of an electronic dictionary affects the learning of a second language.* (February 16, 2011)

This is one of several examples provided by Fernando that calls into question the knowledge and skills of his English instructors. The imposition of seemingly arbitrary rules about the role of electronic dictionaries in the language classroom tends to undermine the legitimacy of the instructor and lower students' motivation to follow the curriculum. Research can be found to support different views on the use of dictionaries in second language classrooms; the question here is: Who decides what is best for the student when there is a range of experience and knowledge in the possession of the adult learner? Where does/should power and authority reside? If the answer (implicitly or explicitly) is that the teacher is the ultimate authority, then this will be reflected in virtually all aspects of pedagogy and curriculum; even more than that, I would argue that the classroom becomes a surrogate for society writ large, wherein authority resides within institutional structures with their rules and regimes of management of people, ideas, processes, and values justified, in the end, as the privileged knowledge of experts with institutional power and the 'right' to exercise their authority justified by their socially sanctioned and recognized 'expertise' (yet another example of how social exclusion operates in everyday life). Another example concerns how an instructor dealt with a student's question on a substantive matter and why Fernando felt that the instructor's attitude undermined his confidence in the instructor's professionalism as a teacher:

> *The English instructor has been trained to teach English. I am not underestimating his knowledge or education, but, unfortunately, his background cannot cover all fields of professions to enable him to discuss with every professional in the group. For example, in one class, one of the students asked him what the difference was between ethics and morals. His answer was: both terms mean the same thing … I told him that it is not the same, there is a big difference in meaning between both terms, but he insisted to me that they mean the same. I tried to explain to him with practical examples but I couldn't convince him and at the end he told me: "No, there is no difference. Both terms are exactly the same for me. Period." I have some teaching background from my profession. From that experience, I consider it very important to help the students to get the right knowledge. For that reason, I don't approve of that attitude.* (February 16, 2011)

What is important to note here is that the instructor has discounted the knowledge of the learner while imposing his own (incorrect) view on the class. This is a clear example of how an instructor's teaching philosophy (transactional) and his or her desire to be the authority ('expert') in the classroom, even on matters not pertaining directly to language learning, may convey a message of disrespect (regardless of the instructor's intention) toward the students in the classroom; it creates an impression in a learner's mind that the learner is ignorant, his or her knowledge is limited (possibly because he or she doesn't come from an English-speaking/educational background), and therefore the learner should keep his or her thoughts to him or herself in the future. Not only does such an approach diminish learner motivation, but it also sends the message to the learner (and the class) that authority and legitimate knowledge resides in the (Canadian) teacher and disagreeing with the teacher is not easily tolerated and probably not worth the effort on the part of the student.

The reason Fernando is enrolled in this course is because he had no other options; nonetheless, he remained in the course, even though he did not see any value in it for him:

> *I wonder how many doctors in the province of Alberta have to write essays? I am sure that if I had the opportunity to get immersed in the medical field and keep listening to the professionals in the field, in six months I would be ready to perform in this field, since I have the medical skills; I just need to improve my language skills. I consider that just writing essays about ridiculous topics, such as 'advantages of having a car' or 'advantages of having a dog' will not benefit me at all. It seems to me that they are either underestimating the knowledge of professionals in the group or trying to make us frustrated to drop the course.* (February 16, 2011)

Despite Fernando's negative view of the goals of this class, he was determined to make it work for him:

> *I was asked to write an essay about the similarities and differences of dogs and cats. Based on my experience and skills I tried to focus my writing on the metabolism between them, to address it to my field. When I showed it to my instructor, he emphasized that he didn't understand my point of view. He said that the way I approached the topic was not clear for him because he didn't know much about the metabolism of dogs and cats and he didn't know if I was telling the truth. He asked me to write something more suitable to the topic. In that case, I had to re-do it mentioning more common things like how dogs and cats communicate and behave or the appearance they have. He finally approved my writing. All that struggle is frustrating for me.* (February 16, 2011)

Maria was also enrolled in a course at a local college in Calgary. She did not experience her English classes in the same way as Fernando, although she did share some of the same concerns mentioned by him:

> *I think it is very difficult for instructors in any college* [College X or College Y], *to manage big groups of students with different backgrounds and levels of English. For example, in the same group there are totally different students: one is a doctor, another is an engineer, the other is a young girl who just finished high school in her home country; others have children while others don't have any, etc. The groups are heterogeneous. Of course the interest in the topic of conversation is completely different for each one.* (February 16, 2011)

The Experiences and Roles of Jose and Eugenia Martinez

Unlike their parents, Jose and Eugenia arrived in Canada with high levels of English proficiency. In Colombia, both Jose and Eugenia were educated from pre-kindergarten through junior high school (Jose) and elementary school (Eugenia) in an English immersion program; students in the program were expected to have high levels of proficiency in English by the time they reached secondary school. In Calgary, Jose has often been called upon to serve as a translator for his parents in meetings with health providers and teachers; for example, when Fernando needed to get a pair of glasses, Jose came along as the interpreter: "We went with our son, since he is our 'official translator.' When we go with him we have no problems" (November 2, 2010). On other occasions, their daughter has served as an interpreter, sometimes accompanied by Jose: "We had a meeting at our daughter's school. Her teacher was kind and helpful. In my case, even though I understand a lot, when I try to speak, I have trouble; therefore, we went with our son Jose; he cooperated with us in the communication ... On some occasions our daughter helps us to communicate as well" (November 2, 2010).

In response to question #9, 'Can you tell us about your children's schooling and your interaction with teachers and school personnel since you came to Canada? How satisfied are you with your children's access to education?' Fernando and Maria expressed concerns about how their children were treated, and about the quality of education in the public school their children attended. They also mentioned the culture of the school, mainly relations between students and teachers, teachers and parents, and differences in patterns of social relations outside of school. On the positive side, Fernando noted

> *Our children have adapted to the education process. An important factor is that they learned English in our country. It was of benefit that we could afford to send them to study in an English immersion school. They have no problem with the language. They didn't need to take ESL courses. They have always received good marks on the English tests.* (November 2, 2010)

When asked about any recent visits either Fernando or Maria had made at their children's school in the past month (Question #8), Maria responded:

> *We had a meeting at our daughter's school. Her teacher was kind and helpful. In my case, even though I understand a lot, when I try to speak I have trouble; therefore, we went with our son Jose; he helped us with the communication.*

At the interview on September 30, 2010, we asked Fernando and Maria about their children's schooling and about their interaction with teachers and school personnel since their arrival in Canada (Question #9). These were, in part, their responses:

Maria: *I think that is okay, and our children are more adapted now.*

Fernando: *Our children have adapted to the education process. What contributed to that adaptation is that they learned English in our country … Regarding the interaction between students, parents, and teachers, there is a barrier. In our country the teacher is a good friend, mentor, and advisor who is always accessible when needed. There is a good interaction between teachers, students, and parents. Here, in Canada, our children have suffered sometimes a kind of discrimination from the teachers because they are Latin American and speak Spanish.* (September 30, 2010)

Beyond differences in the school culture, especially regarding roles and interactions between teachers, students, and parents, both Fernando and Maria complained that Jose's experiences in school were having a negative impact on his educational attainment, and eventually Jose transferred to a high school in the Calgary Separate School District, also known as the Catholic School District; Jose became frustrated with the pace and quality of education and attitudes of some of the teachers at the high school in which he was enrolled. One concern expressed by Fernando was that his son was more advanced in his knowledge than the curriculum in his tenth grade classes:

Fernando: *My children have had a regression in their educational progress. The problem is that they have not been given the opportunity to perform at the right level. My son was registered in grade 10 this year* [2010] *and he is studying topics that he learned back home many years ago. If he were given the opportunity to be in the right grade, he might have been able to finish his high school this year instead of wasting his time repeating what he already knows.* (November 2, 2010)

When he petitioned to have his son placed in 11th grade, he was told that would not be possible because he was too young; Fernando understood the argument and didn't complain. However, Fernando believed that differences in his children's language and cultural background were not properly taken into account, and misunderstandings often resulted:

> *For example, my son had a situation of discrimination in his school because he speaks Spanish and on one occasion he was told that he is mentally delayed. The only way he was able to overcome that barrier was by speaking to the teacher in French, since he knows French as well. My daughter was dismissed from her daycare due to language barriers that originated in a misunderstanding from the caregivers. We wrote a letter of complaint to the respective authorities but never received an answer. They should understand that the attitude and behavior of immigrants is based on differences of language and culture. They shouldn't accuse someone just because of a misunderstanding. I consider that a child has symbolic language and it is the responsibility of adults to find the meaning of what they try to express. We should never assume that a child means what we want or think he/she means. It is what they really want to express.* (November 2, 2010)

Maria: *I think that any staff should understand that our daughter, due to her condition as an immigrant, is in the process of her adaptation. Another important aspect is that they should consider the differences in ways of thinking between immigrants and Canadians.* (November 2, 2010)

As time went on, Fernando and Maria came to understand that approaches to teaching and learning, at least in Calgary, differed in a number of ways compared to their experiences in Colombia. For example:

Fernando: *We realized that the learning process in Canada is more relaxed compared to the exigencies they used to have in Colombia, both in terms of academics and discipline: it is stricter (in Colombia).*

At the interview on February 16, 2011, Fernando discussed a dilemma that he and his son were dealing with about his courses and options at his high school. Both were confused about the policy and expressed uncertainty about what courses Jose should be taking:

Fernando: *Since he (Jose) started his high school, he wanted to take advanced courses. Some teachers advised him to do it but some others didn't. Then he started taking the basic courses and he obtained excellent marks, between 96 and 97% in all of them … He is confused now because some teachers advise him to do it in order to take the modular system of education which would allow him to take the advanced courses faster to save time, but some others tell him to continue in the regular system … I think that it is important that instructors or counselors in the schools provide more consistent information regarding preparation guidelines for students entering university. My son is confused because he has been told that it is exactly the same result if he takes basic or advanced courses. It just depends on the marks he gets, which I think is not true. I think some careers in university require the advanced courses.* (February 16, 2011)

Despite this confusion, in the end Jose did transfer to a different high school and after graduating, enrolled at the University of Calgary. Apparently, the academic preparation that Jose and Eugenia had in Colombia, in terms of academic subjects and academic English proficiency, enabled them to succeed in the Calgary schools. As Maria and Fernando noted:

Maria: *They are not having problems with homework or stressed with the school. Everything is okay for them.*
Fernando: *That's right! Fortunately, school is not difficult or stressing for either of them.*

To summarize, Jose and Maria benefitted from their English immersion programs in Colombia, which allowed them to easily transfer the knowledge they acquired in school in Colombia to their schools in Calgary. However, they still felt penalized as Spanish speakers and as cultural 'outsiders' in a school system, and Canadian society, that was unwilling to accept their cultural—and educational—capital as fully as the capital of 'insiders' was accepted.

Being a Doctor When No One Recognizes Your Profession

Fernando and Maria understood when they arrived in Canada that their lack of appropriate English proficiency would make it difficult for either of them to gain employment in their respective professions. However, as Fernando explained, when he was told "You cannot practice your career in Canada," in large part, "because you don't have Canadian experience," he found such a requirement to be arbitrary and discriminatory, something that went far beyond the matter of competence in English:

Fernando: *I think that Canadians could be physically different (e.g., skin color, eye color, etc.), but illnesses are the same anywhere. Human anatomy is the same for any person. For example, if I am asked to assist a Canadian patient or a Colombian or Chilean, etc., who has an abdominal gun-shot, I know how to proceed based on the human anatomy because it is exactly the same in any person. What I mean is, if I am given the opportunity to perform in my career I would demonstrate my experience! But that is really, really difficult. The medical union in this country is inaccessible. That is incomprehensible! If they allow every professional immigrant to perform a career they will feel replaced. They might think that professional immigrants have a lot of experience and for that reason it could be better for them not to facilitate the opportunities for other professional immigrants.*

There is certainly truth to Fernando's assertion that Canadian professional societies, associations, and guilds exercise control on professional licensure and accreditation, whether in medicine, nursing, engineering, education, or accounting, among other fields, and the reasons are not exclusively based on concerns about protecting the public interest. McDonald et al. (2015, p. S116) analyzed the process of immigrant selection and occupational outcomes of international medical graduates (IMGs) in the United States and Canada. They found that in Canada, where a point system has been in place, "IMGs are less likely to be employed as physicians than are IMGs in the United States, where employer nomination is a more important entry path for IMGs." They also found that "when the point system in Canada did not have occupational restrictions, IMGs have a relatively low probability of working as physicians." While having a profession can enhance an applicant's ability to be granted landed immigrant status, that is, permanent residence, once in Canada, decisions about certification are made in each province by the relevant professional society; in other words, gaining entry into Canada as a physician provides no particular benefit or path whatsoever for gaining licensure as a physician, and in the case of Alberta, the number of IMGs granted residencies, once they meet all of the qualifications in English and the three required exams, is highly restricted. These restrictions and gatekeeping mechanisms also apply to other professions, such as law, engineering, architecture, accounting, nursing, and so on.

McDonald et al. (2015) make a series of calculations based on the 2006 Canadian census on occupational outcomes for male medical degree holders, aged 29–65 in Canada and the United States. The authors (p. S122) found that of those who studied outside Canada (N = 2721), 57.2% are working as physicians, compared to 91.2% (N = 6471) who studied in Canada. In contrast, in the United States, 87.1% (N = 5091) who studied in the United States are practicing physicians, while 73.5% (N = 1628) who studied outside the United States are practicing physicians (p. S122); thus, IMGs are nearly 2.5 times more likely to be practicing physicians in the United States compared to those in Canada. The authors conclude (p. S121), "This is strong preliminary evidence of a much larger problem of finding suitable employment either as a physician or in some other high-skill occupation among IMGs in Canada compared to the United States." Wanner (2001, p. 147) claims that nonrecognition of foreign credentials and prior work experience is the "... central immigration issue of the new century not only in Canada, but in all postindustrial societies receiving immigrants."

The obstacles that Fernando faces appear insurmountable. The likelihood that he will be able to get a license to practice medicine in Canada is extremely low. In the interview of December 9, 2010, Fernando said that he had talked to a Colombian surgeon at a local hospital (he provided the name of the surgeon, who will remain anonymous), who attends surgical transplants, and he told Fernando that his situation would be more complicated because he was a specialist. The Colombian surgeon said that he (Fernando) would have to retrain in family medicine and that could take between four and five years. That retraining would enable him to work as a surgical assistant only, still in the family medicine area. Fernando summarized his situation thusly: "I would be ending that process in the next eight years; by that time, I would be looking for a job when I am a senior and probably 'walking with a cane'" (a common expression used in Spanish to indicate 'old age' or, in this case, something that will happen too late to be useful).

Fernando is frustrated by the lack of opportunities to interact with English-speaking Canadians, by the barriers to getting any type of job, and by the fact that the English classes he can enroll in are mostly inappropriate for his language needs; in addition, he is also effectively blocked from many of the services and benefits that citizens take for granted that might help him improve his financial and social situation. These include the inability to get credit from a local bank in order to start a business, since he doesn't have a job and has no credit history in Canada. Fernando and Maria tried to initiate a business, but they could not obtain bank financing because they have no credit history, and without a job, or record of employment in Canada, they found that starting and sustaining a small business in Calgary was nearly impossible.

Fernando: *It is a bar and restaurant that we want to open. Everything we need for this project is so expensive. Even though people say that in Canada there are facilities to finance small business, for immigrants it is so difficult to be approved with financial assistance. The first requirement we are asked to fulfill is record of credit in Canada, as well as record of employment. Since we are immigrants and we don't meet those requirements it is very difficult, almost impossible, to have a credit approval.* (February 16, 2011)

The only jobs available for immigrants, according to Fernando, "… are cleaning or truck driving, and that doesn't help us" (February 16, 2011).

Another source of frustration and an affront to his dignity is that Fernando's knowledge and experience as a highly trained surgeon is totally disregarded by the medical establishment in Calgary. For example, when his teenage daughter was taken by Fernando to the emergency floor of a local hospital, as a pediatric surgeon, he understood that her symptoms indicated a diagnosis of appendicitis, "… and I told the doctor that she was having appendicitis and the doctor did not believe me; we brought her to the hospital at 8:00 am and she was diagnosed and not taken to surgery until 1:00 am the next day" (November 2, 2010). In Colombia:

> … *if any of my children got sick, they were seen with priority by my colleagues. Here it is the opposite; my daughter has been sick for two weeks now and the doctor didn't prescribe anything; even though I know what her problem is, I*

cannot do anything because I cannot get the right drugs for her without a prescription; that makes the situation more difficult. (December 9, 2010)

Fernando did meet, finally, with representatives of the Alberta Medical Association (AMA) who are in charge of reviewing accreditations of applicants to practice medicine in the province; he realized that it would be almost impossible to fulfill the requirements they stipulated and that it would take four to five years to complete them. Fernando was informed in his conversation with a representative of the AMA that he would need an overall score on the Test of English as a Foreign Language (TOEFL) of 95–100 (out of a possible 120 points) and a subscore in listening of 25 (out of 30). It is completely unrealistic for Fernando to achieve these high scores; of greater concern is whether the TOEFL is the best measure to assess Fernando's English ability to practice medicine in Canada, since it is generally used for admission into tertiary educational institutions and is normalized on that population. There is no doubt that Fernando's English needs to improve, but without any opportunities for gaining access to the professional contexts that are relevant for the practice of medicine, even a 'good' score on the TOEFL exam might not indicate whether or not Fernando has sufficient proficiency in the appropriate discourses for his profession. As Fernando explained:

> *I really wish to have the opportunity to perform in the medical field, just the way I used to do. I was in the hospital environment for almost twenty years and I consider that my life. I would like to have the opportunity, at least, to observe the situation in this environment and practice my listening and speaking skills in the medical language, but that is impossible for me. It is very difficult to be accepted, especially in my field. One of my instructors told me that the procedures I used to do in my career are done only by two surgeons in Calgary; they are the only ones who operate on newborns and pre-mature newborns in this city … She encouraged me to talk to them. I already contacted one of them through his e-mail and requested an interview, not with the purpose of getting a job but to practice. Even though I explained to him what I did, e.g., different surgeries and laparoscopies, he wasn't interested … I expected to have more opportunities, but I realize that professionals here are not open to help.* (November 2, 2010)

When Fernando hears that 'Canada has the highest standards of health in the world,' he considers that "to be just a theory." To illustrate his skepticism, he related the situation of his sister, who had recently been diagnosed with breast cancer and had to wait for a few months for treatment. When we interviewed him on November 2, 2010, Fernando noted:

> *If she were in Colombia, by this time she would have had her surgery and treatment. Here, she has been waiting for several months, going from here to there. She will get her surgery when she has a metastasis or more complications or when it is not treatable anymore. I don't understand what is happening if they say that Canada has the highest standards of health.* (November 2, 2010)

It took two months to confirm that there was something abnormal. After that it took a month to perform a biopsy. A month later they told her the results and after that she had to wait another month for surgery. Another source of anxiety and frustration, both for Fernando and his sister, is that Fernando is not given complete information as to the nature of the tumor; when the hospital called his home (where his sister is living), he was informed by the nurse that her chemotherapy would start on December 20, but nothing else. When Fernando spoke with the surgeon at the hospital, he tried to get more information on the type or stage of the cancer, explaining that he (Fernando) was a surgeon, but the surgeon would not provide any information (December 9, 2010). Fernando compared the situation in Canada with that in Colombia:

> *In my country, it is different. If I am seeing a patient and I know there is a relative who is a doctor, this is a major reason to be open and to provide information. That facilitates closeness between the doctor and the patients' relatives. By medical ethics we know that relatives of a doctor have priority. That is established by the professional ethics. Here, that is the opposite.* (December 9, 2010)

In these examples, it wasn't only a language barrier that frustrated Fernando, but rather the humiliation he experienced by the total erasure of his identity and expertise as a highly trained pediatric surgeon who only wanted to provide important information about his young daughter's medical condition and to get more particular and precise information on the medical status of his sister. In fact, Fernando has come to realize that it is better "not to mention that I am a doctor because that immediately creates a barrier" (December 9, 2010).

With the modest financial support that the federal government provides to Fernando running out, with little prospect for obtaining a license to practice medicine of any type—let alone as a certified neonatal surgeon—with no ability to borrow money to start a small business (he opened a small restaurant that is open on weekends only, but barriers to access to credit have made it impossible to sustain the business), and with the language barrier still a major factor in all aspects of his daily life, including interactions with his children's teachers, Fernando has seriously considered returning to the dangers of Colombia rather than continuing to live under current conditions:

> *If I had imagined even 5% of this reality, I would rather have taken the risk of being killed over there [Colombia] rather than enduring the situation in which I find myself.* (December 9, 2010)

He has applied for positions in some hospitals in Panama City, and has even considered the possibility of volunteering for two weeks in Haiti in order to maintain his skills; but without money, he couldn't afford to go to Haiti. Even though returning to Colombia would involve a high risk of being kidnapped again or killed if he didn't meet the ransom demands, Fernando reasoned:

> *Despite all of the dangers that we might face back in Colombia, I think that it is better to take that risk given all of the frustrations we have experienced here. At least we would have the opportunity to have our careers and a decent life in our country ... The way we are living here we feel as if we have lost our dignity while we have to beg for help in order to survive.* (December 9, 2010)

Despite being close to despair when we spoke with Fernando in December 2010, in our interview with him and his family on January 12, 2011, Fernando was much more upbeat about his prospects. He told us that he had the opportunity to speak with native English speakers and that he had improved his communication skills and had greater confidence:

> *I am not afraid anymore to go to do things by myself, like going to the bank or shopping at the supermarket, making a telephone call to an office or attending an appointment. I do it myself and am able to communicate in English 80 to 90%.* (January 12, 2011)

After considering a career in nursing (which would have required retraining, additional tests, and financial hardship), Fernando decided that his best option was to take a course to qualify as a Pharmacy Technician at a local college; he subsequently completed the course and is currently employed at a drug store chain in Calgary. His children were doing well in school, and his son enrolled as a full-time student at the University of Calgary; his daughter will likely attend university in Canada as well. His children's future prospects are bright, and this is a source of pride and optimism for Fernando and Maria. His wife continues to improve her English skills as well. She is optimistic about her ability to resume a career in accounting:

Maria: *I have been told that if I get a benchmark of 8 (in English), I would be able to take a training in Accounting for Immigrants which is an accelerated program in ten months, but my teacher said that it would be better to take all the modules of the (English for Academic Purposes) course that is two more modules. In that case, after I finish this one, I will take eight more months of English to be able to start the Accounting course which takes ten months.* (February 16, 2011)

While the program in accounting will not qualify Maria for accreditation as a Chartered Public Accountant (CPA) in Canada, that is, the equivalent status she had in Colombia, she is hopeful that the courses offered at Southern Alberta Institute of Technology (SAIT) in Oil Accounting will lead to a job in the lucrative energy sector in Alberta.

Conclusion

When people move across national borders in search of better economic and social opportunities, often traversing great distances, it is inevitable that they will face many challenges. With regard to matters of language, Blommaert (2010, p. 6) notes, "Movement of people across space is … never a move across empty spaces. The spaces are always someone's space, and they are filled with norms, expectations, conceptions of what counts as proper and normal (indexical) language use and what does not count as such." Those who move from a place in which their language is dominant to a place in which it is not dominant, or even recognized, will find their identity and status challenged in unexpected ways (Blommaert 2008). These observations apply in the case of Fernando and Maria, whose deficiencies in English have impacted their ability to integrate into mainstream Anglophone Canadian society on their own terms, that is, as professional, highly educated individuals with a strong desire to contribute to their adopted country, Canada, in the professions for which they are qualified with decades of experience. However, while language proficiency is an important index of one's social capital in a particular time and place, what counts as proper and normal educational, professional, and experiential capital in those spaces is also dependent on the norms, expectations, and conceptions of the people who already inhabit those places, and especially those people with the authority to adjudicate the value of credentials and the worthiness of life histories that may fall outside the 'normal' patterns and expectations.

Certain types of social capital traverse frontiers more easily because of compatibility of language/language variety, cultural traditions, and socio-economic standards of living; however, professionally credentialed highly skilled immigrants and refugees face significant barriers to resuming their careers in Canada because large professional associations (e.g., the College of Physicians and Surgeons and the Alberta Medical Association) have implemented rules and requirements for accreditation that tend to under-value (or even not recognize) credentials, training, and/or work experience of immigrants from particular, and especially non-Anglophone, countries in the case of Alberta; for example, as was previously discussed, the number of IMGs who will be admitted into Medical or Surgical Residency positions in the province of Alberta has been limited in recent years to about 10% of all positions available. In Colombia, Fernando was a highly respected and successful neonatal surgeon, while in Canada he was hard-pressed to get a job as a janitor, and he is resigned to the fact that he will never be able to practice his profession while in Canada. Passing the required written exams for medical licensure is not a problem for him with regard to the content or the language (English) of the exams; in fact, he has already taken the first exam (in English) and easily passed it. However, the exams are very expensive, and once he has passed the first two written exams, he must pass a third, oral exam, wherein he is expected to interact with patients (played by actors), and will be evaluated according to a standard equivalent to that of a student graduated from a Canadian medical school. But beyond these hurdles lies the problem that his advanced medical training in his specialty must be repeated. Another issue faced by Fernando is what physicians call 'recency' of practice: by being a non-practicing physician for multiple years while living in Canada, Fernando's clinical skills have eroded which creates yet another barrier to resuming his career or the careers of similarly situated IMGs. In the final analysis, Fernando came to accept the reality of his situation and found his best option was to become a Pharmacy Technician: it had some connection to his professional training and it was a relatively affordable and obtainable goal. It wasn't simply due to the language barrier and the lack of appropriate and affordable language training that led to Fernando's decision to accept a career path for which he was highly overqualified, but rather because Canada was not and is still not able to successfully facilitate the integration of tens of thousands of highly trained professionals that arrive each year into the careers that they had before arriving in the country. Immigrants of all categories (e.g., economic class, family class, government-sponsored refugees, and refugee claimants) eventually find employment because of their determination to succeed as new Canadians by accepting almost any job in order to support themselves and their families, including jobs with limited potential for upward socioeconomic mobility. Institutional rules, regulations, customs, and societal attitudes play equally important roles in limiting the options these highly educated refugees have to practice their professions in Canadian society (see the discussion of 'social exclusion' in Chap. 2). The experiences of the Martinez family revealed in this chapter provide a rich 'thick' description (Geertz 1973) of how these barriers are experienced in the everyday world of work and education, and how members of the Martinez family dealt with these barriers and challenges, often in creative ways that are not captured by government aggregate data, such as rates of employment participation, and school graduation rates among the children of refugees and other classes of immigrants in Canada. An important insight revealed in the experiences of the Martinez family is the way that cultural and linguistic difference is stigmatized, often through invocation of stereotypes, and the negative impact of these attitudes on the classroom experiences of adult English language learners whose individual agency and self-worth is undermined, with negative consequences on their self-esteem and, ultimately, their ability to resume their professional careers in Canada, or to pursue new career paths. The most important deficit revealed by the experiences of the Martinez family resides with Canadian society writ large; how can a multicultural, democratic, immigrant-receiving country address this deficit so that the experiences of the Martinez families of the future will not be a repeat of the Martinez family of today? We will address this dilemma in Chap. 6.

Notes

1. All names used in this chapter are pseudonyms.
2. Fernando's mother and four brothers were living in Canada at the time of the interviews; his three sisters decided to remain in Colombia, and two other brothers still living in Colombia have applied for government-sponsored refugee status and their applications were in process at the time of the interviews. All of Maria's relatives remain in Colombia.
3. According to Dr. xxxx, Department of Family Medicine, University of Calgary, in the province of Alberta the Alberta Medical Association (AMA) sets aside a percentage of places (i.e., a quota) for International Medical Graduates for residencies; the quota is around 10%, so that if there are 100 residencies available in a given year, around 10 are allocated for IMGs; therefore, the system is not based on a merit system within the pool of applicants, but rather on a bifurcated system in which IMGs compete with other IMGs within their allocation of 10% of the total applicants.
4. In the interview on January 12, 2011, Fernando said that he took a course in Medical Communication at a local community college that helped him with medical terminology for interviewing patients. He also indicated that he wanted to take another course online that is oriented to prepare medical reports or requests.
5. In *Emotions and Multilingualism* (2005), Aneta Pavlenko explores the role(s) that emotion plays in the learning/acquiring and use of a second language, an area of research that has often been overlooked in the pervasive 'monolingual' research paradigm that predominates in the second language acquisition research literature.

References

Bauder, H. (2003). "Brain abuse", or the devaluation of immigrant labour in Canada. *Antipode*, 699–717.

Blommaert, J. (2008). *Grassroots literacy: Writing, identity and voice in Central Africa*. New York: Routledge.

Blommaert, J. (2010). *The sociolinguistics of globalization*. Cambridge: Cambridge University Press.

Cervatiuc, A. and Ricento, T. (2012). Curriculum meta-orientations in the LINC program. *Canadian Journal for the Study of Adult Education*, 24(2): 17–31.

Geertz, C. (1973). The Interpretation of Cultures. New York: BasicBooks.

Historical Memory Group. (2013). *Enough already! Colombia: memories of war and dignity*. Bogota: The National Center for Historical Memories (NCHM).

McDonald, T., Warman, C. & Worswick, C. (2015). Immigrant selection systems and occupational outcomes of International medical graduates in Canada and the United States. *Canadian Public Policy* 41, Supplement 1, August, S116–S137. Toronto: University of Toronto Press.

Norton, B. (2000). *Identity and language learning: Gender, ethnicity, and educational change*. London: Longman.

Pavlenko, A. (2005). *Emotions and multilingualism*. New York: Cambridge University Press.

Wanner, R.A. (2001). Diagnosing and preventing "brain waste" in Canada's immigrant population: A synthesis of comments on Reitz. *Journal of International Migration and Integration*, 2(3), 417–28.

CHAPTER 5

Patrick and Chantal

Abstract In this chapter, we hear the stories of a married couple from the Democratic Republic of the Congo. Patrick, 47 years old, had a good life as a businessman in the informal economy of a low-income, African country until the onset of war and threats to his and his wife's security required that they leave the country and come to Canada as government-sponsored refugees. His wife, Chantal, 47 years old, has not been able to obtain permanent resident status after trying for more than ten years. Patrick's experience as a small businessman in Congo is not recognized or valued in the formal, credentialed, and salaried economy of Canada, whereas Chantal cannot work because she lacks appropriate legal status.

Keywords Republic of the Congo • Refugee claimant • Bureaucratic barriers • Permanent residence status • Quebec • French • Social network • LINC program

The other two individuals whose stories will be related in some detail are a married couple from the Republic of the Congo. Patrick,[1] 47 years old, had a good life as a businessman in the informal economy of a low-income, African country; with aspirations for a better life in another country, he decided to try his luck in Canada and arrived in Quebec, Canada, in 1993, as a refugee claimant. Following the outbreak of the civil war in Congo, which began in 1997, his future wife, Chantal, fled to Quebec, Canada,

T. Ricento, *Refugees in Canada*,
https://doi.org/10.1007/978-3-030-76453-1_5

seeking asylum as a refugee claimant. Patrick obtained permanent resident status in 2001; he applied for Canadian citizenship in 2006 but because he had moved to a new address, and he did not receive documents to proceed with his application from the Canadian government, he had to reapply in 2009 and at the time of the interview, he was hopeful he would gain citizenship status in the near future. In contrast, his wife Chantal[2] has lived in Canada for nine years, eight of those years in Montreal before arriving in Calgary. They have four children, ranging in age from ten months to seven years of age. Although Patrick had much less formal education than Fernando when he arrived in Canada, his inability to borrow money from a bank necessary to buy a truck to become an independent businessman resulted in a severe diminution of his ability to use his skills and knowledge to participate in the Canadian economy. His wife, Chantal, 37 years old, has not been able to obtain permanent resident status after trying for more than ten years, even though her spouse (Patrick) had been a permanent resident since 2001. The stress of not obtaining permanent resident status, which barred her from many social services (including full medical coverage, among other benefits she did not qualify for) and prevented her from getting a job, led to serious mental anguish, resulting in a period of hospitalization. In the Congo, even poor people can enjoy a rich social support network, something that does not exist for Patrick or Chantal in Calgary.

Life in the Democratic Republic of the Congo

Patrick and Chantal both left the Congo for similar reasons: to escape the civil unrest that escalated into a devastating war. They both arrived initially in Quebec because their fluency in French gave them an advantage they hoped would ease their integration into Canadian society.[3] All of the adults from the Congo in our study were refugee claimants, that is, they had not applied for refugee status in their countries of origin, as was the case with the Martinez family (Chap. 4), but rather applied for residence status as refugee claimants after they had arrived in Canada; therefore, unlike the members of the Martinez family, who were given permanent residence status upon their arrival in Canada as government-assisted refugees, this 'limbo' status created problems for Patrick and Chantal; for example, the legal documents that are required by the government to process refugee claimant petitions, such as birth certificates, marriage licenses, and passports, are generally not available to refugees who have not been processed prior to their arrival in Canada. Despite long delays and other hurdles to obtaining permanent resident status in Canada, both Patrick and Chantal were appreciative of how laws work in Canada, in stark contrast to the situation in Africa:

Patrick: *... I like how laws work here in Canada; everything is governed by law ... it is different in my country ...: in Africa, if you have money you can buy laws, you can make your own laws and you can do whatever you want, but here in Canada everybody is equal. [However], it is frustrating in another way when you are waiting for your immigration papers you are not allowed to work; for example, Chantal was not allowed to study English because of her legal (undocumented) status.* (August 30, 2010)

Patrick became a permanent resident (PR) of Canada in November 2001, and so he was able to have the same benefits as any other permanent resident, which includes nearly the identical social services benefits, including health care and access to most employment, as Canadian citizens; the main difference is that PR cannot vote in provincial or federal elections. However, at the time of the interview, Chantal still did not have her PR card, although she did have a work permit, but with her limited English skills she felt her job options were limited (her goal was to become a nurse in Canada). As a refugee claimant, she was not eligible for full medical benefits that are available to all permanent residents and citizens.

While Patrick and his wife are grateful to be in Canada, they have had to endure extensive bureaucratic barriers to gaining permanent residence status (Chantal) and citizenship (Patrick); they consider these delays to be unfortunate even though they respect the legal processes that contrast sharply with their experiences in Africa. Both Patrick and Chantal have found that life in a country like Canada, where adherence to the law and a commitment to equality under the law, is to be expected, means that many things are possible for them and their children that were inconceivable in Africa:

Patrick: *I would say 'yes' (in answer to the question whether he was satisfied with the way his immigration case has been handled so far), even if it takes a long time and it is also very complicated, but I like how laws work here in Canada; everything is governed by law ... which means there is peace and peace is guaranteed everywhere. It is also frustrating in other ways; when you are waiting for your immigration papers, they don't allow you to work, and when*

> *Chantal asked for a study permit so that she can learn English, immigration refused without any reason. Immigration said first find a school which will accept you and then come back and ask immigration for the necessary papers. It is complicated and it looks like it is the immigration agents who are making those decisions.* (October 7, 2010)

Lack of proficiency in English has contributed to other barriers in gaining work for both of them; for example, in the case of Patrick, his experience as a small businessman in a developing, low-income country (Congo) is simply not recognized or valued in the formal, credentialed, and salaried economy of Canada, whereas Chantal is limited in the work that she qualifies for because she lacks appropriate legal status, and doesn't have sufficient proficiency in English for most jobs that would be relevant for her career aspirations in the medical field.

Before the civil unrest started, Patrick was able to enjoy a decent lifestyle in the Congo. He rented a small house downtown and had his own business, selling vegetables and preparing fast food for restaurants (e.g., sandwiches). However, conditions began to worsen in the period leading up to the civil war; he saw people being killed in front of his eyes and dying of starvation. Due to the lack of safety and transportation, people could not even go to the hospital:

Patrick: *The great difficulties and challenges back home was war; before war … I could survive and there were not lots of difficulties. With small business in the street, like buying vegetables here and selling them there, you can live without any problem.* (August 30, 2010)

Patrick's knowledge of Canada prior to his arrival was limited; yet he believed that as long as he could live in peace in a democratic country, he would be able to fulfill his dreams:

Patrick: *When I first heard about Canada I was at school … when you are still young, you have some kinds of dreams: I will become a doctor, I will go to this place or other. That is why I decided to travel (i.e., to leave the Congo when he was young, prior to the war there).* (August 30, 2010)

He came originally to Quebec mainly because as a Francophone he believed he and his future wife would have more opportunity for education and a bright future. After he obtained permanent resident status in

Quebec, he went to a technical college in Montreal and got a two-year degree in engineering. However, he was not able to get a job even after looking for five years; instead, he did odd jobs, working for various social services agencies that help families to readjust to life in Canada. The fact that he was a fluent Francophone living in the only Canadian province in which French is the *sole* official language did not 'level the playing field' for him. As a visible minority, and as an 'outsider,' fluency in French did not provide any apparent advantage. Eventually, he moved west to Alberta, hoping to find more opportunities to work in the field for which he was trained.

After three years in Calgary, Patrick and his wife were struggling, living on $900 per month[4] for all expenses, well below the official poverty level; they also depended on a local food bank to make ends meet. While Patrick and Chantal both appreciate the safety and security that living in Calgary affords, and believe in the principle that everyone should be treated equally and fairly, their status as refugees limits their access to the kinds of benefits, services, and job opportunities that citizens, especially native-born Canadians, expect and take for granted. They do not like being dependent on government support and charity in order to survive. Robert has continued to try to find work that will enable him to support himself and his wife:

Patrick: *I tried to do my best, like renting a big truck and look for a market in transportation companies, work by myself, but it was very difficult. I contacted DHL, FED EX … it was very difficult … rent a car for $1500, gas, insurance. I could not afford all those things … Now my future life in Canada, I am still looking for it ….* (October 7, 2010)

The stress of their circumstances contributed to hospitalization for Chantal who had been experiencing psychological problems; as Patrick recounted,

Patrick: *… when she (Chantal) arrived here (in Montreal), immigration said that you cannot get papers even though your husband sponsored you, but the sponsorship doesn't count, so she had to wait. It is stressful if you don't have papers. We tried even to get a lawyer who can intervene so that she can at least get a health card, but that doesn't work … These (events) caused my wife to be disturbed mentally and she got admitted for mental problems to the hospital due to the stress.* (October 7, 2010)

Eventually, thanks to the intervention of the Women's Association in Calgary, Chantal was able to get her Alberta Health Care card. However, at the time of our interviews, she had not yet received her permanent resident card ten years after applying for it, and she has no idea when she will get it:

Chantal: *when I make a call (to the immigration authorities) they say that my case is pending, just be patient ... so I don't know how long it is going to take ...* (August 30, 2010). *Without permanent residence, I am nothing, I don't have any rights ... because I am not in social service, I don't have a right to get a lawyer or a judge ... I don't have a right to work and I never apply for it.* (November 23, 2010)

Another resource that was available in Congo that is not available in Canada is the social network and community support system that enabled Patrick and Chantal to persevere during difficult times in their lives. As Chantal described it,

Chantal: *In the Congo, even if there is poverty, there is also something better, like living in that society. There people are not closed in their houses, not like here where you are like isolated and like you are living alone. But there all people are outside, either you have or don't have food, but you are outside; sometimes somebody has a potato in his hand, he can give it to you, and every-body say 'hi' and how are you doing, whether you know him/her or you don't, and if you are sick you will say 'No, I am not doing well," and that person will inform any person he/she will meet and say "I said hi to someone and he/she said that I am sick"; everyone will come and say 'we heard that you are sick,' and if you don't have food, they will bring some. Moreover, if you have kids, you cannot suffer. You can leave the kids to anybody who is available there. We don't have daycare because we can't pay for it.* (August 30, 2010)

Because free ESL classes are available through the LINC program only to immigrants who have permanent resident status, and Chantal is ineligible to enroll in the subsidized LINC program, she cannot afford to pay for English classes, nor can she find work due to limitations in her English skills. As Patrick rather succinctly put it:

Patrick: *You are like in an open prison. You see others living, but you are not living. As soon as you are living that situation, it finally makes you sick.* (October 7, 2010)

Patrick also noted that some people who arrive in Canada illegally, circumventing the legal processes, are able to stay in the country, while he and his wife have played by the rules and are still in limbo. When they hired a lawyer, he took their money and went to France. Without financial resources to hire another lawyer, with difficulties in communicating effectively with bureaucrats in Edmonton (location of the provincial capital in Alberta) and Ottawa (the federal capital city) orally or through e-mail, and without social support networks that they had been accustomed to in their home country to provide psychological and social support, the freedom and security of Canada offers little solace. Asked how he hoped his life in Canada would be ten years from now, Patrick replied:

Patrick: *I expect to have peace, I expect to get a job, take care of my kids, open their own accounts. I don't worry because I am still alive … If you don't have a job, you don't have peace. I remember when I was in Montreal, my wife got sick and I decided to quit my job, so that I could take care of my kids; with that condition, you don't have peace. All that is caused by immigration … that stresses us and is affecting our whole family, it keeps us in poverty … you cannot move forward.* (October 7, 2010)

Conclusion

An important difference in the experiences of the Martinez family compared with those of Patrick and Chantal is that the Martinez' could rely on their extended family—mother, sister, brothers—for emotional and psychological support during their transition to life in Canada, support which was not available to Patrick and Chantal; support provided through closely knit social networks has been shown to positively affect measures of well-being among refugee populations in Canada and elsewhere (see Chap. 3 for discussion). For refugees like Patrick and Chantal, with less formal education and training than Fernando and Maria prior to their arrival in Canada, but who had decent lives in their countries of origin, often made possible by work in the informal economy, finding a foothold in a society organized by bureaucracies and institutional hierarchies that require particular sorts of evidence necessary to allow a person to gain access to most social goods (e.g., proper birth certificates, school transcripts, letters of reference from past employers, credit reports necessary to borrow money), poses obstacles that are invisible to most native-born Canadian citizens. For a *bricoleur* such as Patrick, with his real-world knowledge and work experience gained in the Congo, combined with his two-year engineering degree obtained in Canada, and proficiency in French (an official language in Canada), something as basic as getting a credit card proved to be a herculean task; yet, without the ability to develop a credit history, he could not borrow money necessary to start a small trucking business that would give him a chance to have a better life. And without the social support networks that he and his wife depended on in the Congo to see them through difficult times, the psychological stresses they both experienced due to problems with their legal status and downward economic mobility, became more problematic over time.

Limitations of space prevent me from providing additional details about the lives of Fernando, Maria, Patrick, and Chantal and their encounters with school system bureaucracies, housing, and transportation issues, along with many other challenges, and how their current disempowered status has affected their children's lives. Nonetheless, the details provided convey the essential point of this and the previous chapter, which has been to illustrate the ways in which the involuntary diminution of social and cultural capital that the Martinez family and Patrick and Chantal have experienced has contributed to a sense of powerlessness in their respective lives, severely limiting possible and realistic paths to a normal life that each had hoped to recapture in moving to Canada. Their resilience in the face of adversity speaks to their strength of character that has enabled them to maintain hope when despair seemed like the only possible option. The governments (federal and provincial) of Canada have provided them with at least some resources and opportunities to improve their situation,[5] but what these refugees require more than government aid is broader societal recognition and validation of their considerable skills, training, and experiences so that they can become fully engaged citizens in Canada, with the same rights and responsibilities as other citizens, which includes equal access to employment and the social goods and services that their earned social and cultural capital should entitle them to.

In the final chapter of this book, I will consider shortcomings to the argument that the Canadian government, through its policies and good intentions, has done about as much as can—or should—be expected, under these circumstances. I will discuss some positive changes in policy along with additional options that could improve the challenges faced by refugees, such as those experienced by Fernando, Maria, Patrick, and Chantal; some of these options can be achieved if there is the political will to do so; however, other options are aspirational and would require a profound rethinking of what is meant by words like ‘citizenship’ and ‘equality’ along with a more critical engagement with Canadian multiculturalism and a better understanding of how language is *the* crucial variable affecting the integration of refugees and other classes of immigrants in Canada today.

Notes

1. A pseudonym.
2. A pseudonym.
3. French is the only official language in Quebec and is often required for careers in the province.
4. This is the amount provided to them by the federal government.
5. For example, permanent residents in Canada are eligible for 1200 hours of free ESL instruction for a period of up to three years.

CHAPTER 6

Challenges and a Way Forward

Abstract In this chapter, I summarize the core challenges that have been identified in the literature on immigrant and refugee resettlement, not only in Anglophone countries but also in other countries in Europe and elsewhere. I discuss how the economic motives of receiving countries tend to overshadow and underfund programs and services for refugees and other immigrants seeking better lives. The effects of proficiency in an official language in Canada (English or French) are discussed, along with other factors identified in the research literature, that tend to be associated with professional de-skilling, resulting in underemployment, as well as lower rates of labor market participation among various groups of refugees and immigrants, often leading to downward socioeconomic mobility.

Keywords Social exclusion • Point system • Foreign credentials • Ontario Human Rights Commission • Occupational standards • Immigration policies • Language programs for immigrants • Canadian Language Benchmarks • Enhanced Language Training • Hidden curriculum

I begin this chapter by summarizing the core challenges that have been identified in the literature on immigrant and refugee resettlement, not only in Anglophone countries but also in other countries in Europe and elsewhere that receive relatively large numbers of immigrants and refugees

T. Ricento, *Refugees in Canada*,
https://doi.org/10.1007/978-3-030-76453-1_6

each year. There are commonalities in the goals of immigration and resettlement policies in these countries, with comparable effects on the lives, livelihoods, and general well-being of immigrants and refugees. In this review, I will bring into focus how the economic motives of receiving countries, such as Canada, tend to overshadow and underfund programs and services for refugees and other immigrants seeking better lives; here, Marx's definition of alienation (see Chap. 2) becomes particularly relevant as it pertains to the experiences of immigrants and refugees whose earned cultural and social capital is not recognized (as in the case of Fernando and Maria in Chap. 4, and Patrick and Chantal in Chap. 5), leading to a reduction in social status and a downturn in socioeconomic mobility; in addition, their resources in 'non-official' languages are ignored, or even viewed as detrimental to integration in the receiving society, and their unfamiliarity with the norms and 'rules' of the host society places them at a further disadvantage as they seek recognition by a society that makes much of its commitment to human rights, 'multiculturalism,' 'multilingualism,' 'anti-racism,' 'gender equality,' and other progressive values that are claimed to be important aspects of national identity.

In a study of the integration of refugees into the European education and labor market, Seukwa (2013) found that newcomers are systematically excluded socially, resulting in a sense of isolation, leading many refugees to describe their experiences in the host society as "living in an open prison" (Seukwa 2013, p. 12). That same sentiment was shared by Patrick (this book, Chap. 5) in describing his and his wife Chantal's living situation in Calgary. Without permanent residence status, Chantal feels socially and emotionally excluded from Canadian society:

Chantal: *Without permanent residence, I am nothing, I don't have any rights … because I am not in social service, I don't have a right to get a lawyer or a judge … I don't have a right to work and I never apply for it.* (November 23, 2010)

When asked how he hoped his life in Canada would be ten years from now, Patrick expressed how his life, and that of his family, has been impacted by immigration to Canada:

Patrick: *I expect to have peace, I expect to get a job, take care of my kids, open their own accounts. I don't worry because I am still alive … If you don't have a job, you don't have peace. I remember when I was in Montreal, my wife got sick and I decided to quit my job, so that I could take care of my kids; with that condition, you don't*

> *have peace. All that is caused by immigration … that stresses us and is affecting our whole family, it keeps us in poverty … you cannot move forward.* (October 7, 2010)

In describing the factors that led to his wife's hospitalization in Calgary due to the many stresses she had endured, including the inability to attend English classes or to work because of her legal status as a refugee claimant (despite being married to a Canadian permanent resident), Patrick put it succinctly: "You are like in an open prison. You see others living, but you are not living. As soon as you are living that situation, it finally makes you sick" (October 7, 2010).

Canada has made significant changes to its immigration policies in recent years; for example, while in 1992, the federal government allocated 12 points (out of 100) to educational level, in 2006 that was increased to 25 points; in 1992, 15 points were allocated to special vocational preparation, while zero points were allocated in 2006; knowledge of French or English received 15 points in 1992 and 24 points in 2006; adaptability had zero points in 1992 and 10 points in 2006[1] (Kaushal and Lu 2014: 283). Yet, many studies have shown that immigrants' labor market outcomes have declined over the last several decades, even though their average level of education is higher than that of the Canadian-born population (e.g., Hawthorne 2008). Despite the Canadian government's attempts to increase the number of skilled workers (including those with professional credentials) admitted each year,[2] nonrecognition of foreign credentials, education, and experience continues to work against the economic goals of federal immigration policy; Reitz, Curtis, and Elrick (2014) use census data to present a calculation of losses due to both lower earnings for immigrants and less access to skilled employment. In constant 2011 dollars, they estimate that these aggregate losses to the Canadian economy rose from $4.80 billion in 1996, to $6.02 billion in 2001, to $11.37 billion in 2006. Some attempts at the federal and provincial level have been made to eliminate unnecessary barriers to accessing registration and licensure (Jantzen 2015, p. S50). Ontario was the first province to pass fair access legislation and the Ontario Office of the Fairness Commissioner has been working to ensure that unnecessary access barriers are reduced, if not eliminated, by requesting that regulatory bodies provide rationales for why a requirement is necessary (p. S50). The Ontario Human Rights Commission (2013) has questioned the Canadian experience requirement for registration since that requirement contributes to the systemic disadvantage of internationally educated applicants and therefore raises human rights concerns (p. S50). The intergovernmental Forum of Labour Market Ministers (FLMM) developed the Pan-Canadian Framework for the Assessment and Recognition of Foreign Qualifications in 2009 in order to ensure "a fair and competitive labour market environment where immigrants have the opportunity to fully use their education, skills and work experience for their benefit and for Canada's collective prosperity" (FLMM 2009). While Pan-Canadian occupational standards have been adopted in most of the Framework's target occupations (19 professions and 4 trades are included in the Pan-Canadian Framework), the Framework merely aims to notify an individual within one year "… whether their qualifications will be recognized, or be informed of the additional requirements necessary for registration, or be directed toward related occupations commensurate with their skills and experience" (p. S51); in other words, the Framework acts primarily as an information clearinghouse that merely informs immigrants and refugees whether their professional credential meets the already existing requirements for registration and licensure in regulated professions. While better than nothing, these steps do not address the more important matter of why professional degrees earned outside of Canada, and why non-Canadian experience, are automatically suspect and can be summarily rejected by professional credentialing bodies throughout the country.

Besides problems in accessing the workforce, immigrants and refugees experience many other problems that result in varying degrees of social exclusion; Wayland (2006) found that legal and policy barriers to settlement are interconnected and tend to produce systemic discrimination against immigrants, refugees, and refugee claimants, among others. These barriers can lead to isolation and lack of civic engagement. This situation of social exclusion has been found to exist in other receiving countries, including Australia (Taylor 2004), the United States (Brown and Scribner 2014), and many European countries as well (Seukwa 2013). Although proficiency in the dominant national language is not the only factor that influences successful integration into the workforce, it is clearly an important factor; in the interviews with the refugees that form the core data for this book, lack of appropriate skills in English was mentioned by virtually every person we interviewed as a major barrier to finding a good job, to obtaining accreditation in their profession or skilled trade, to effectively communicating with service providers, and to feeling comfortable communicating with Canadians and feeling part of Canadian society. Therefore,

I will now turn to the role of language in the integration process for refugees and immigrants, an area in which a great deal of research has been conducted but without having much of an impact on the design and delivery of effective language instruction in programs for immigrant and refugee newcomers in diverse contexts in Canada.

While I will be focusing on the Canadian context in the following discussion, it is (again) worthwhile to note that the Canadian situation, with regard to the apparent goals of language programs intended to help newcomers integrate into the Canadian workforce, is not unique. The same market-driven approach that has led to major changes in immigration policies in recent years in Canada is also evident in other immigrant-receiving countries, with commensurate implications for language programs in those countries. In particular, there is a focus on providing language programs designed to prepare adult immigrants and refugees for entry-level, low-wage jobs, with little differentiation in curricula that fail to account for the diverse educational backgrounds (including levels of literacy in their primary language), professional training and credentials, and prior work experience outside Canada; in addition, accessibility for many clients is limited because of conflicts with work schedules, because affordable child care is unavailable, and because of long waiting times for many newcomers to get into Language Instruction for Newcomers to Canada (LINC) programs,[3] among other reasons. Most classes do not provide enough instructional hours to achieve anything but token gains in proficiency, and programs designed for learners who hope to re-establish their professions in Canada are virtually nonexistent (see the case of Fernando in Chap. 4). But Canada, as I have mentioned, is not unique in its approach and capacity to deal with the language needs of immigrants and refugees. Immigrants in Norway are expected to reach a functional level of language competence in Norwegian after about 250 hours of language instruction; a similar emphasis on basic language skills for low-paying jobs are to be found in the Elementary Swedish Language Program for Adult Immigrants in Sweden, the PanHellenic Project on Greek in Greece, and Portuguese programs in Portugal that aim to develop basic literacy skills after 200–300 hours of instruction (Li and Sah 2019, p. 330). The available research on typical rates of learning a foreign or second language demonstrates that the number of classroom contact hours required to achieve adequate levels of competence in the four skills most skilled jobs require—listening, speaking, reading, writing—far exceeds the hours provided in language programs for newcomers in the large immigrant-receiving countries, which include (in addition to the ones already mentioned) Germany, the Netherlands, the United Kingdom, Australia, and Spain (Gramling 2009).

The criticisms about the programs discussed above are supported by data on program attendance, course completion, and achievement of program goals. For example, in Australia, a survey of the Adult Migrant English Program (AMEP) found that only 30% of the clients completed the 510 hours of required training; 7% achieved the required level; and 34% had zero English language skills training (Department of Education and Training Australia 2015). In Canada, according to a Citizenship and Immigration Canada (CIC) report, in Canada's LINC program, out of 55,286 participants only 19,162 completed the required 500 hours of training in 2009 (CIC 2009).

In the following paragraphs, I will discuss the findings from a research project conducted in Calgary that examined the effectiveness of programs funded under the 'Enhanced Language Training' (ELT) initiative, launched by the federal government in 2003 to provide a higher level of language instruction to enhance the ability of immigrants and refugees to integrate into the Canadian workplace. While the LINC program is designed to provide basic language instruction to adult newcomers in one of Canada's two official languages (English and French), and to help them to become acculturated to the 'Canadian way of life,' the ELT program was designed to reach persons with more years of education, including those with professional and skilled trade credentials, and with advanced English Language Proficiency (ELP), as measured by the Canadian Language Benchmark (CLB) scores; typically, these programs are geared to the communication needs of a specific profession, and they include a workplace component as part of the cultural and language development of English for professional purposes (EPP) (Watt et al. 2007). The research project I will be discussing was conducted during the early years of the ELT Program and there may have been improvements in the programs over the past decade or so; however, the sorts of issues raised in the study, including the very modest improvements made in English language proficiency as measured by comparison of pre- and post-test scores on measures of speaking, listening, reading, and writing, are likely to still exist in many, if not most, ELT programs offered today throughout Canada.

Watt et al. (2007) note that "the goal of ELT programs is to identify the kinds of oral and written communication that are expected in the profession and then to develop a language program to address those language expectations, through a range of authentic interactions introduced in classroom practice and extended through structured work placements where the genuine interactions occur." There is no standardized national curriculum, nor are there any specific measurable performance objectives for these programs; rather, individually funded programs are expected to develop appropriate curricula, materials, and assessment tools along with developing ties with employers in the local area who are willing and able to provide opportunities (at no cost to the employer) for students in the program to spend time at the workplace in order to have an opportunity to be immersed in an authentic environment in the professional field in which they aspire to work in the near future. Watt and his team worked with a total of eight institutions that offered ten different programs in Alberta, including:

- International Engineer Bridging Program
- International Pharmacy Bridging Program
- Enhanced Language Training for Skilled Immigrants in Engineering
- Enhanced Language Training for Internationally Trained Professionals
- Business Communications for Professionals
- English for Skilled Immigrants (ESI)
- Skills for Employment and Lifelong Learning (SELL)
- Transitions to Technical and Trades Careers
- Practical Nursing Diploma for Internationally Educated Nurses

They collected the following data and information: (1) interviews with program managers, instructors, and learners; (2) program and curriculum documentation; and (3) language proficiency data on the students prior to and following the program of instruction.

Based on interviews and document analysis, Watt et al. (2007, Executive Summary) identified key issues in the ELT programs included in the study:

1. In general, ELT programs do not share an equally developed sense of vision regarding the purpose and direction of their mandate.
2. The relationship between the classroom component and the workplace component in ELT programs is still largely underdeveloped. None of the programs integrated instruction in professional language proficiency into their workplace component. Most programs

viewed the workplace component as a stand-alone item that had little to do with the program's instructional intentions and was generally difficult and time-consuming to arrange. In at least one case, no workplace component was offered, in contrast with the publicly stated goals.

3. Not all programs demonstrated a strong connection to employers and/or the professional associations related to their program focus. Such a connection would strengthen the language and professional development goals of work placements as well as providing strong curriculum support for the selection of professional communication tasks for instruction.
4. The issue of language assessment within ELT programs is an area that could benefit from extended discussion. A large number of the ELT program managers and instructors questioned the validity or utility of the Canadian Language Benchmark Assessment (CLBA) and Canadian Language Benchmark Placement Test (CLBPT) assessment measures. Other programs created their own in-house assessment instruments or alternate formal assessment processes that may not necessarily reflect the goals of measuring professional language proficiency.

In terms of results on gains achieved in English language proficiency, from a total of 267 possible participants, paired scores (pre-class/post-class) for 149 were available for analysis. Based on results of either the CLBPT or the CLBA, average benchmark gains per 400 hours of classroom instruction were quite modest: Speaking 0.64/Listening 0.60/ Writing 0.58/Reading 0.52. Students who began the program with higher levels of English proficiency experienced smaller gains compared to those who entered with lower proficiency (reflecting a 'ceiling effect,' not a surprising result). To put these findings in the simplest terms, an average of about 400 hours of classroom instruction results in an increase of approximately one-half (0.52) a benchmark for writing, to nearly two-thirds (0.64) of a benchmark for speaking, with listening and reading between these two values. To achieve an increase of 1 benchmark or more requires approximately 1300–1500 hours of instruction for the four measures (Watt et al. 2007, p. 67). Perhaps as important is that the scores on the CLBPT or the CLBA do not measure professional language proficiency as those tests measure general language proficiency[4]; whether the participants gained proficiency in the language of their profession was not directly measured. However, as noted in point 2 above, none of the programs integrated instruction in professional language proficiency into their workplace component; most programs viewed the workplace component as a stand-alone item that had little to do with the program's instructional intentions. Taken together these findings suggest that much work needs to be done in terms of program and curriculum development, in teacher training, and in the development of working relations with private sector companies that have the time and desire to fully buy into the vision and goals of the ELT program.

I turn now to research on LINC programs in Canada. The Canada Employment and Immigration Commission created LINC in 1992 with the mandate of providing "basic language instruction to adult newcomers in both official languages and to facilitate the settlement and integration of immigrants and refugees into Canadian society" (Citizenship and Immigration Canada 2003, p. 6). Research strongly indicates that most LINC programs are geared toward the passive *adaptation* of immigrants and refugees rather than their *integration* into Canadian society. Freire (2005, p. 4) makes a philosophical distinction between integration and adaptation; according to Freire, adapted people are passive, domesticated, and adjusted "objects" who tacitly accept the sociocultural norms of the dominant group, while integrated people are subjects or agents capable of making personal and social changes and who create, recreate, and participate in their historical epochs.

LINC instructors throughout Canada have access to an online competency-based curriculum document (LINC 1–5 Curriculum Guidelines (Toronto Catholic District School Board, 2002)); these guidelines include 'Topic Development Ideas,' 'Strategies for Learners,' 'Resources for Developing and Teaching Topics,' 'Topic Outcomes,' and 'Sample Tasks.' Beyond these very general guidelines, instructors have a great deal of latitude in terms of the content of their course and the manner in which that content is delivered in the classroom. Because of the indeterminate nature of what is taught and how it is taught in LINC classrooms, Cervatiuc and Ricento (2012) focus on the *hidden curriculum* defined by Giroux and Penna (1983, p. 102) as "the unstated norms, values, and beliefs that are transmitted to students through the underlying structure of meaning, in both the formal content as well as the social relations of school and classroom." Viewed in this way, "… the LINC program is positioned within the larger context of Canadian society and conceptualized as an agent of socialization rather than solely a language-learning program" (Cervatiuc and Ricento 2012, p. 18). Cervatiuc and Ricento's (2012) study of a LINC program in Calgary consisted of interviews with nine LINC instructors, observations of classes taught by the instructors, examination of curriculum documents, teaching materials, and other resources available to instructors. Based on analysis of the teacher interviews and classroom observation of their teaching methods, Cervatiuc and Ricento (2012, p. 26) found that six of the nine instructors demonstrated a transmission approach to teaching Canadian culture, which is essentially descriptive: "A transmission approach identifies, presents, and explains various aspects of Canadian culture. It simply informs learners about the Canadian ways of doing things … and provides descriptive information about geography, food, shopping, etiquette, and famous people (e.g., Wayne Gretzky). 'We learned about hockey, because hockey is an important part, and they know now who Wayne Gretzky is now, because that is an important part of Canadian culture'" (LINC 3 male teacher). As the authors note (p. 26): "Students are basically expected to retain information and imitate Canadian models in order to fit into society. The hidden curriculum that results from advocating the imitation of dominant cultural models promotes symbolic violence (Bourdieu and Passeron 1977) or the imposition of thought and perception by dominant agents upon dominated agents." An alternative to the transmission approach to teaching identified by Cervatiuc and Ricento (2012) is the participatory transformation approach to teaching Canadian culture that was observed in only one of the classes they observed in the study. In that class, "students were asked to compare the impact of various aspects of culture on their past and current lives. By engaging students in a critical dialogue and analysis of the similarities and differences between their own cultures and Canadian culture, students became more aware of their current circumstances and were encouraged to act as agents of their own lives" (p. 26). While a transmission model of teaching Canadian culture promotes adaptation rather than integration, a participatory transformation approach views students as subjects who go through a process of integration, rather than mere adaptation, and are encouraged to develop the critical ability to make social and personal changes[5] (pp. 26–27).

Previous research indicates that the hidden curriculum of ESL (English as a Second Language) schools in the United States tends to socialize immigrants and refugees to be docile, have low expectations, and internalize failure (Morrow and Torres 1998). Curry (2001) analyzed the hidden curriculum of adult community college ESL writing classes in the United

States; at the classroom level, it promotes passivity and focuses on grammar, pronunciation, and isolated language skills. Students are expected to give the facts and select 'nice' or unproblematic writing topics. They are penalized for thinking critically and expressing different opinions. Immigrants tend to be viewed as a monolithic group, where individual histories and future goals are disregarded. The economic layer of the hidden curriculum inculcates conformity and the 'cooling out' of immigrants' professional aspirations so they can be retained in the low-paying labor force. The unstated message is that it does not matter how qualified immigrants might be (as doctors or engineers, for example); they have to start afresh, have low professional expectations, and be happy with their status quo (in Cervatiuc and Ricento 2012, p. 21).

Cray (1997) conducted interviews with six teachers in Ottawa and observed a few classes to gauge teachers' perception of the LINC program, including the curriculum; Cray's findings indicate that teachers do not consider the LINC curriculum as having much impact on their teaching practices. Most of them occasionally 'flipped through' the document to get ideas of topics to cover; Cray found that "for these teachers, the document was too detailed and long to be useful" (p. 33). In other research conducted in Canada, Morgan (2002) argues that identity should be viewed as an integral part of the curriculum and that classrooms should be integrated into the broader sociopolitical context of society. Morgan's position is that a critical ESL teacher is one who helps learners develop language skills that challenge inequitable power relations beyond the classroom; to achieve that goal, Morgan advocates a participatory teaching model in which learners see themselves as partners who discuss issues relevant to their lives.

Recall the efforts made by Fernando (Chap. 4) to choose a writing topic in his English for Academic Purposes (EAP) class that would allow him to demonstrate his medical knowledge, and the reaction of the instructor who told him to write on a topic that he (the instructor) could understand because he couldn't evaluate the truthfulness or accuracy of an essay that compared the metabolisms of cats and dogs; also recall Fernando's attempt to question the instructor's claim that 'ethics and morals are the same thing'; the instructor insisted that his position was absolutely correct and there was no opportunity provided by the instructor for a discussion that would have given Fernando an opportunity to demonstrate his knowledge on the subject and that would have shown respect for his intellect and experience. Fernando's patience in writing an essay on a topic that the instructor approved was commendable, but in his interview, he expressed his great frustration with the narrow-mindedness of the instructor and the uselessness of writing on a topic he felt was ridiculous. Fernando also questioned the relevance of writing essays on assigned topics about which he (or many of his classmates) had no interest, among other concerns he expressed about the teacher's classroom policies, such as forbidding the use of electronic dictionaries based on nothing more than the teacher's arbitrary personal view. While Fernando granted in his interview that the teacher had qualifications and experience that he (Fernando) lacked, Fernando also understood that the classes he was enrolled in were simply not relevant to his goal of advancing his English language skills sufficient to enhance his ability to gain entry into the medical profession in Canada:

Fernando: *I wonder how many doctors in the province of Alberta have to write essays? I am sure that if I had the opportunity to get immersed in the medical field and keep listening to the professionals in the field, in six months I would be ready to perform in this field, since I have the medical skills; I just need to improve my language skills. I consider that just writing essays about ridiculous topics, such as 'advantages of having a car' or 'advantages of having a dog' will not benefit me at all. It seems to me that they are either underestimating the knowledge of professionals in the group or trying to make us frustrated to drop the course.* (February 16, 2011)

The research that has been discussed in the preceding paragraphs is in line with Fernando's experiences, especially his comments on the content and pedagogical approaches he was exposed to in his LINC and other English classes in Calgary. As a confident, highly educated professional person who only wanted to be able to continue in his career as a pediatric surgeon, support his family, and contribute economically and socially to his newly adopted country, Fernando was often perplexed by the seemingly arbitrary and unreasonable barriers to improving his English that he encountered; perhaps most disturbing in the case mentioned above is the insensitivity of at least one instructor who (apparently) failed to understand that because a person may not be a highly fluent speaker in one language (English), and that he is a 'learner' of English and also a refugee from a particular country (Colombia, in this case), he nevertheless has much to contribute to the learning process for his own benefit and for the benefit of others in the class, including the instructor. The asymmetry in power relations in the classroom allows such uninformed, largely unconscious views to manifest themselves in ('hidden') curricular choices, classroom teaching methods and styles, teacher-student interactions, and assessment of learning, with often quite devastating effects on the students whose marginalized and vulnerable status places them at a disadvantage when confronted with unreasonable demands and negative evaluations of their intellectual mettle; all too often, the negative effects of these types of asymmetrical power relationship that involve persons who provide important services, such as instructors in LINC programs, can lead to frustration, withdrawal, and resignation (recall the previously discussed data on low program attendance, course completion rates, and achievement of program goals of English programs for immigrants and refugees in Australia and Canada). Students in many of these programs in Canada and other Anglophone countries 'vote with their feet' since their voices are silenced.

Conclusions

Our research findings, based on analysis of extensive interviews with members of six refugee families in Calgary, are concurrently validated by a large body of published research reviewed in this book that enumerates the barriers experienced by newcomers in their desire to integrate in their host country; for both refugee and non-refugee immigrant groups, the most pressing goal which affects all other aspects of their lives as newcomers, is to obtain satisfying and sustaining employment. Refugees arrive in Canada with educational levels, skills, experiences, and abilities that are not unlike the skills and abilities of other classes of immigrants who were admitted under the economic class or family-class categories; the main difference is that both government-assisted refugees and asylum seekers (refugee claimants) have fled their home countries because they were facing extreme persecution based on their beliefs (religious, political, cultural), threats to their personal safety due to war and/or terrorism, environmental catastrophes, among other reasons, while economic and family-class immigrants have chosen to emigrate specifically to Canada for personal reasons (which could overlap with those of refugees to varying degrees), often waiting many years in their country of origin for their application for admission to be processed and finally approved. On average, Canada has offered permanent residency to about 250,000 immigrants and refugees from more than

190 countries each year over the past decade (CIC 2017). Between 2011 and 2016, 60.3% were granted permanent resident status through the Economic Immigration Program, 26.8% arrived under the Family-Class Program and 11.6% were refugees. While the process of arriving in Canada differs between these programs, and there are differences in some of the characteristics of the people who arrive based on their entry program (see Chap. 3 for discussion), the research presented in this book clearly demonstrates that the experiences of all categories of newcomers to Canada have commonalities that lead to similar outcomes over time in terms of their experiences in the labor market.[6] Particularly revealing were data on the experiences of immigrants whose academic and professional credentials were earned abroad, discussed in detail in Chap. 1.

Ultimately, the effects and consequences of policies, practices, beliefs, and attitudes about and toward all categories of immigrants affect not only the lives of immigrants and their families but the lives of all Canadians. Although an important goal of immigration policy is to raise the standard of living of all Canadians, prominently mentioned in the Immigration and Refugee Protection Act (2001), little research has been conducted on the impact of immigration on the Canadian economy. However, available data suggests that immigration policies have not 'lifted all Canadians' economically in part because underlying problems with the economy cannot be adequately dealt with by simply importing new workers to satisfy short-term labor needs in specific sectors of society; as Lightman and Good Gingrich (2012, p. 125) note "… the gap between Canada's rich and poor not only persists, but has increased more rapidly than ever in the past three decades (Fortin et al. 2012; Osberg 2008; Yalnizyan 2009). Since the mid-1990s, both inequality in household earnings and numbers of people living in poverty have risen faster in Canada than in any other OECD country (OECD 2008)" (see endnote 6, Chap. 2 for details).

In an analysis of research focusing specifically on the labor market outcomes of immigrants in Canada, Picot and Sweetman (2012, p. 5) note that "… in many immigrant-receiving countries, the labour market outcomes of all categories of new immigrants have declined appreciably. Canada is no exception. This is probably one of Canada's major social policy conundrums, and it has occurred in spite of rapidly rising educational attainment among new immigrants." In their review of the literature, Picot and Sweetman (2012, pp. 7–8) find there are many factors involved in explaining the relative entry earnings of successive cohorts of immigrants; however, they argue that the most important factor accounting for earnings differentials is language skills "… which appear to have a direct effect on labour market outcomes as well as influencing the rate of return to formal education. Immigrants with good language skills in English or French can more easily convert their education to earnings than those without such skills." Picot and Sweetman (2012, p. 8) cite the research of Goldmann, Sweetman, and Warman (2011) who found that "… language ability affects the return to educational credentials, with language ability being particularly important for those with higher levels of education." As I have argued in this chapter, language programs conceived and subsidized by the federal government and developed in partnership with provincial and local NGOs and other institutional providers have had limited success in delivering appropriate and sufficient language instruction for newcomers. Cervatiuc and Ricento (2012) argue that the teaching methods, curricular content, and expectations of teachers in LINC and ELT programs reflect a 'hidden curriculum' that relies on prescriptive 'transmission' of Canadian culture as a fixed idea to which students should passively accept and adapt to. Other shortcomings of these programs were revealed in the research of Watt et al. (2007) that demonstrated problems in the delivery of specialized (ELT) language programs due to (among other reasons) a lack of a clear vision as to the goals of the program, nonexistent or ill-defined partnerships with local professional societies/employers, and unrealistic expectations about what is required to enable students in these programs to achieve their goals in terms of appropriate and sufficient language skills required to enter the workforce in their desired profession.

While the components of settlement policies and goals in Canada are multilayered with many types of diverse local programs designed to promote the successful integration of immigrants,[7] it seems that language continues to be perhaps *the* central issue upon which other factors hinge. Recall Dell Hymes' comments in Chap. 2 that asked researchers to "… go beyond a liberal humanism that merely recognizes the abstract potentiality of all languages, to a humanism which can deal with concrete situations, with *the inequalities that actually obtain, and help to transform them through knowledge of the ways in which language is actually organized as a human problem and resource*" (italics added). Hymes understood language as enacted interpretative behavior that occurs in real time that can create and reinforce asymmetric power relations by speakers of different languages/language varieties, indexed to differences in social status, race/ethnicity, gender, age, national origin, among other possible differences.

Understanding the powerful role that language plays in the experiences of immigrants needs to be better understood by policy makers and program developers who are likely to view language learning as a fairly straightforward process of 'acquiring a skill'; the experiences of people like Fernando, and the other refugees interviewed in the study presented in this book, provide insight into the emotional and psychological costs of being a limited English speaker in English-dominant Canada.

Possible Changes in Policy(?)

After considering the many factors that must be considered in the development of policy in Canada regarding the earnings potential of immigrants, which include levels of immigration, the business cycle, occupational labor shortages, and regional distribution of immigrant resettlement, among other factors, Picot and Sweetmen (2012, p. 1) recommend several reforms to immigration policy, including:

> reducing immigrant inflows during recessions, selecting younger immigrants, continuing to emphasize language skills, placing employer-sponsored immigration within the context of the longer-term goals, maintaining the focus on highly skilled immigrants (those in the skilled trades as well as college and university graduates) and supporting continued economic success among the children of immigrants.

While these authors do not discount the importance of humanitarian motives as important elements in immigration policy, their recommendations, if adopted, could have serious consequences by prioritizing recruitment of immigrants with the most desirable current and potential economic capital while downplaying the humanitarian dimension that has enabled tens of thousands of refugees and other categories of immigrants to land in Canada whose sociodemographic profiles would be seen as less desirable in a system that views immigrants (including refugees) principally as 'economic units' with variable potential performance outcomes in the labor market. In fact, these types of recommendations would essentially write-off the chances for many of the adult refugees we interviewed for this book to have meaningful jobs—let alone careers for the most highly educated refugees—given their average ages, lack of familiarity with Canadian culture and lack of Canadian work experience, along with inadequate levels of English proficiency necessary for meaningful employment opportunities in their areas of expertise.

Shields et al. (2016, p. 5) note that the literature on public policy related to immigrants, settlement, and integration makes a distinction between "immigrant" policy and "immigration" policy:

> The former is used to describe the governmental decisions that concern immigrants that reside in the host country, for example, issues around such areas as affordable housing, access to social services, and employment search. Immigration policy, by contrast, refers to the regulation of the flow of people wanting to enter the country. (Shpaizman 2007)

Policies that determine and regulate the flow of people who enter Canada are influenced by politics and economic conditions, which are subject to change and reflect, in part, the experiences of immigrants and refugees in Canada over time, and especially their relative success in entering the workforce and being fully employed and socially integrated. The research discussed in this and previous chapters indicates that the experiences of immigrants of all classifications have exposed major shortcomings in the effectiveness of resettlement policies and practices, including ongoing problems with the validation of foreign-earned educational credentials and the continued and frequent requirement of Canadian work experience necessary for meaningful employment in the areas in which newcomer immigrants are most qualified. Perhaps the most important finding is the relationship between proficiency in an official language and earnings; since the large majority of immigrants in recent decades arrive from non-English-dominant countries (Quebec has control over provincial immigration policy that encourages immigration from Francophone countries), the policy change that could most improve the future prospects of immigrants in terms of employment, career opportunities, and social integration is in the area of language education for newcomers; this is true not only for programs for adult language learners but for their children enrolled in public schools as well.[8] Research presented in this chapter suggests that major reforms in types of programs available, accessibility to programs that take into account the living situations of newcomers, along with changes in curricula, teacher preparation and training, approaches to assessment, and funding levels and duration, among other reforms, could enhance the motivation and, thereby, outcomes of students enrolled in these programs; however, there are other issues that need attention that have to do with expectations of Canadians, who have always played a central role in how newcomers experience their various journeys integrating into Canadian society. For example, do Canadians (especially employers) expect newcomers from non-Anglophone countries to develop and display high levels of English language proficiency in the limited time available in LINC programs to acquire such proficiency? To what degree does 'foreignness,' indicated by how Canadians react to 'foreign accents,'[9] along with 'foreign ethnicity, customs, culture,' limit options for newcomers, not only in obtaining jobs but in being accepted as bona fide Canadians? The research reported in this book has identified visible minority status as an important factor accounting for differentials in levels of employment and earnings among various groups of immigrants. Policies alone cannot effectively deal with these challenges; yet beliefs and attitudes about immigrants (and especially with regard to attitudes toward people identifiable by their racial, ethnic, and/or linguistic characteristics) do exist, not just in Canada but in other immigrant-receiving countries, and those attitudes play as much (or even more) of a role in determining whether or not—and to what degree—immigrants will successfully integrate into, and be fully accepted, by the majority groups in the society. In my view, the essential dilemma facing all actors—including policy makers—involved with improving immigrant outcomes in Canada centers on how the term 'integration' is understood and taken up by a receiving society: attitudes about integration strongly influence not only all aspects of federal, provincial, and local immigrant policies and practices, but also how individual members of the society react to and deal with immigrants, especially those from 'nontraditional' source countries. Shields et al. (2016) define integration as "… the ability to contribute, free of barriers, to every dimension of Canadian [/host society] life, that is economic, social, cultural, and political … [and] if the immigrant wants to participate actively in the society there should be no systematic barriers preventing them from doing so." Since the understanding of the term 'integration' is variable and context dependent, measuring the specific economic and social situations of different populations of immigrants over time is currently the best concrete gauge we have to determine whether, and to what degree, 'integration' (as it is defined in the previous sentence) has taken place. The weight of the existing relevant research reported in this book provides compelling evidence that systemic barriers to successful integration of immigrants continue to exist; correlations between different variables provide some insight into the significance of factors identified through statistical analyses; however, these factors need to be carefully interpreted in order to understand the underlying ('hidden') factors that are not always obvious, such as the actual experiences of immigrants in their daily contacts and interactions with members of the general public. The stories of the refugees (in their own words) recounted in Chaps. 5 and 6 in this book provide greater texture and details on those actual social experiences, including emotional states of mind, that are at least as significant as the statistical data on rates of employment and earnings. It is not that the role of citizens in the integration process of newcomers in the receiving country is ignored or denied; rather, that role is not sufficiently understood or revealed in data compiled by the government; one result of this lack of scrutiny is that greater responsibility (and blame) tends to be placed on the newcomers for their 'own' failures and shortcomings, rather than seeking answers that place equal responsibility on the society for negative outcomes,[10] leading to proposed remedies that focus on characteristics of the immigrants (e.g., linguistic, educational, cultural, and experiential) rather than looking inward at the characteristics and behaviors of individual Canadian citizens.

The Immigration and Protection Act (1991) states that a key goal of the legislation is "to promote the successful integration of permanent residents into Canada, while recognizing that integration involves mutual obligations for new immigrants and Canadian society." A key question raised by the research reported in this book is 'to what extent is Canadian society fulfilling *its* obligation to promote the successful integration of all classes of immigrants?' For example, is Canadian society more porous, more accepting of racial, cultural, religious, and linguistic diversity today than it was when Prime Minister Mackenzie King, in 1947, gave a speech in parliament in which he announced that the policy of the government was to increase the national population by encouraging immigration, while also warning that 'the people of Canada do not wish, as a result of mass immigration, to make a fundamental alteration in the character of our population' (Haque 2012, p. 32)? Five years later, in 1952, the government announced annual quotas on Indian (15), Pakistani (100), and Ceylonese (50) immigrants that remained in place until 1962 (Haque 2012, p. 33). Changes in immigration policies in 1962 removed the quotas from 'undesirable' countries, but as was discussed in Chap. 2, even in the 1960s Canada was being characterized as a binational country that was comprised of two 'founding races' (White Anglophones and Francophones), essentially ignoring the just claims of Indigenous peoples as the 'original founding race,' while lumping all 'other' inhabitants into the 'multicultural' category, an undifferentiated group of immigrants and their descendants whose languages and cultures were (at best) of secondary importance and viewed as irrelevant to successful nation-building.

The idea that Canada has but two languages and cultures worthy of official recognition, with the status that confers, sits uncomfortably with Canada as a multicultural society, if 'multi' means more than two cultures and languages, and if official multiculturalism is meant to be more than a politically correct slogan.[11] Silverstein (1996) describes this approach to defining a nation as a *monoglot ideology*, a concept which rests on the belief that a society is in effect monolingual, coupled with a denial of practices that point toward factual multilingualism and linguistic diversity.[12] Ideologies are more than abstractions; they have real-world consequences on social attitudes and behaviors. Ricento (2013b) notes that the focus on "the existing state of bilingualism and biculturalism" in Canada and the continued dominance of English and French as *the* Canadian languages has tended not only to marginalize the status of 'other' cultural groups and their languages within Canada, but it also presents an image of Canada, to itself and the world, that did not reflect reality in the 1960s, prior to the Canadian doctrine of multiculturalism, any more than it reflects the rapidly changing demographic and linguistic complexity of the country today in the 'post-multiculturalism' era.[13]

Canadian society, historically and in the present day, has operated within an assimilationist ideological framework in which monolingualism (predominately 'standard' English) and monoculturalism (predominately the values and beliefs associated with a White/European/Christian settler society) constitute the baseline norms which 'non-Canadians' should adapt to if they expect to become 'Canadians' (whether or not such adaptation means they will truly be accepted as 'Canadians' by the dominant majority in the 'host' country).[14] The research of Hymes and Labov discussed in Chap. 2, along with a great deal of research reviewed in this book, demonstrates the effects of these ideologies on 'others' whose ethnicities, ascribed racial categories, languages, and 'non-standard' language varieties have placed them in the margins of society, at a disadvantage in a labor market that devalues their 'foreign' education, credentials, and work experience, even though such marginalization runs afoul of the 'official' tropes that claim multiculturalism/interculturalism, anti-racism, and equality of opportunity to be foundational values in liberal Western democratic states (such as Canada). If interculturalism and multiculturalism are to be more than one-way streets in which 'others' are expected to conform and assimilate to 'Canadian' societal norms (impossible for visible minorities) while 'society' does little or nothing to accommodate, respect, support, and learn from the diversity of cultures and languages that enrich and expand the sociocultural compass, then the social and economic challenges facing immigrants in Canada described in this book have little chance of being overcome, despite official efforts through the tweaking of policies to improve the situation; this is because such efforts do not address the deeper problems and obstacles that work against achieving substantive change, namely, the ideologies of cultural assimilation and societal monolingualism, foundational principles of the Canadian national ideology, mythology, and identity.

Notes

1. Adaptability points could be awarded for spouse's education, previous study in Canada, previous work in Canada, arranged employment, and relatives in Canada (Kaushal and Lu 2014, p. 483).
2. Many countries, such as Canada and Germany, have made significant changes in their immigration policies specifically designed to address their short-term labor market needs and shortages (Alboim and Cohl 2012).
3. In Canada, the waiting time for newcomers to get into LINC and other language programs ranges from four months to two years (Li and Sah 2019, p. 332).
4. The goal of the CLB framework is to establish coherence and consistency by 'describing and measuring, in a standard way' immigrants' language and communication abilities (Pawlikowska-Smith 2005). The focus is on what language users can do with the English language rather than their professional knowledge of a particular content area (Gibb 2015, p. 257).
5. Relevant here is Auerbach's (1992) model of the participatory ESL curriculum which draws on the theoretical principles of andragogy (Knowles et al. 1984), which is "the process, methods, and techniques used to teach adults. Andragogy differs substantially from pedagogy ... used to teach children ... because adults learn differently and for different purposes. Adult learners need to know why they have to learn something before they learn it, be responsible for their own learning decisions, be involved in curriculum choices, and be given credit for their life experiences, which represent their richest resource for learning" (Cervatiuc and Ricento 2012, p. 20).
6. There are notable exceptions to this general finding; for example, while the earnings of family-class immigrants were higher than those of refugees during the first full year in Canada (for both men and women), after 15 years

in Canada, refugees from the former Yugoslavia, Poland, and Colombia had earnings higher than their family-class counterparts entering during the same period. Refugees from countries such as China, Pakistan, Afghanistan, Somalia, Iraq, and Ethiopia earned substantially less than family-class immigrants, even after 15 years in Canada (Picot et al. 2019, p. 24).

7. Meinhard and Hyman (2012) employ a complex-system perspective to analyze the Canadian partnership model for immigrant integration and inclusion.
8. Ricento (2013a) demonstrates the shortcomings of programs designed for English language learners in public schools in North America in which monolingually normed approaches to pedagogy and assessment with linguistically diverse student populations are detrimental to their academic achievement.
9. See John Baugh (2000, 2020) who has conducted groundbreaking research on the use of linguistic profiling in hiring practices, education, and law enforcement (among other domains) in the United States and other countries; and Rosina Lippi-Green (2012) whose classic book *English with an Accent: Language, Ideology and Discrimination in the United States* shows how discrimination based on accent supports and perpetuates social structures and unequal power relations.
10. Refer to the work of William Labov (Chap. 2) for a parallel example in the United States in which African American children were blamed for their poor academic performance in school because they spoke a 'non-standard' variety of English (AAVE: African American Vernacular English) which many educators and researchers defined as 'illogical' and 'ignorant,' and the cause of (or a symptom of) cognitive impairment. Labov demonstrated that AAVE was a legitimate variety of English and that it was the responsibility of schools to provide appropriate curricular programs to facilitate the acquisition of the 'standard' English variety used in schools rather than demoting the legitimacy of AAVE and, thereby, its speakers as being 'non-logical' thinkers.
11. One of the goals of the 1971 Multiculturalism Policy was "own group maintenance and development" (Berry 1998, pp. 84–85) while encouraging the learning of official languages (French and English). However, in the 1988 Multiculturalism Act, the focus shifted to the importance of the rights of Aboriginal peoples, the equality of all Canadians, and equality of opportunity, regardless of race, national or ethnic origin, and color. The shift of focus from integration to assimilation is based on assimilationist assumptions (Li 2003) in which it is expected that immigrants give up their native languages, move away from ethnic enclaves, and adopt a Canadian way of life.

12. Although the province of Quebec is the only province or territory in Canada in which French is the sole official language, English predominates in the rest of Canada in which about 75% of the total population speaks English as their first official language, with about 24% speaking French as their first official language (Statistics Canada 2007).
13. See Ricento (2013b) for an in-depth discussion on the current state of multilingualism in Canadian society.
14. A definition of culture was provided in the Report of the Royal Commission on Bilingualism and Biculturalism (Volume 4 (1969, p. 11)): "Culture is a way of being, thinking, and feeling. It is a driving force animating a significant group of individuals united by a common tongue, and sharing the same customs, habits, and experiences. It is a style of living made up of many elements that colour thought, feeling and creativity, like the light that illuminates the design of a stained glass window ... This definition is applied essentially to the two dominant cultures of Canada, those of the francophone and anglophone societies; to a certain degree it also fits the other cultures in this country."

References

Alboim, N. and Cohl, K. (2012). *Shaping the future: Canada's rapidly changing immigration policies*. Toronto, ON: The Maytree Foundation. Available at: <https://maytree.com/wp-content/uploads/shaping-the-future.pdf>

Auerbach, E. (1992). *Making meaning, making change: Participatory curriculum development for adult ESL literacy*. McHenry, IL: Center for Applied Linguistics (ERIC) and Delta Systems, Inc.

Baugh, J. (2000). Racial identification by speech. *American Speech* 75 (4), 362–364.

Baugh, J. (2020). *Linguistics in pursuit of justice*. New York: Cambridge University Press.

Berry, J. (1998). Official multiculturalism. In J. Edwards (Ed.), *Language in Canada* (pp. 84–101). Cambridge: Cambridge University Press.

Brown, A. and T. Scribner. (2014). Unfulfilled promises, future possibilities: The refugee resettlement system in the United States. *Journal of Migration and Human Security* 2 (2), 101–120.

Bourdieu, P. and J.C. Passeron. (1977). *Reproduction in education, society, and culture*. London: Sage.

Cervatiuc, A. and T. Ricento (2012). Curriculum meta-orientations in the LINC program. *Canadian Journal for the Study of Adult Education*, 24 (2), 17–31.

CIC (Citizenship and Immigration Canada) (2009). *Language instruction for newcomers to Canada: Client profiles and performance indicators* [pdf]. Ottawa: Immigration, Refugees and Citizenship Canada. Available at: www.cic.gc.ca/english/pdf/research-stats/LINC-indicators.pdf

CIC (Citizenship and Immigration Canada). (2017). *2017 Annual Report to Parliament on Immigration*. Ottawa: Government of Canada.

Citizenship and Immigration Canada. (2003). *Understanding LINC—Language instruction for newcomers to Canada: A manual and resource guide for service providing organizations*. Ottawa: Canada.

Cray, E. (1997). Teachers' perceptions of a language policy: "Teaching LINC". *TESL Canada Journal* 15 (1), 22–37.

Curry, M.J. (2001). Preparing to be privatized: The hidden curriculum of a community college ESL writing class. In E. Margolis (Ed.), *The hidden curriculum of higher education* (pp. 175–192). London: Routledge.

Department of Education and Training Australia (2015). *AMEP evaluation*. Melbourne: Department of Education and Training Australia.

FLMM (Forum of Labour Market Ministers) (2009). *A pan-Canadian framework for the assessment and recognition of foreign qualifications*. Gatineau, QC: Human Resources and Skills Development Canada.

Freire, P. (2005). *Education for critical consciousness*. New York: Continuum.

Gibb, T. (2015). Regimes of language skill and competency assessment in an age of migration: The in/visibility of social relations and practices. *Studies in Continuing Education* 37 (3), 251–266.

Giroux, H. and Penna, A. (1983). Social education in the classroom: The dynamics of the hidden curriculum. In H. Giroux & A. Purpel (Eds), *The hidden curriculum and modern education* (pp. 100–121). Berkeley: McCutchan Publishing Corporation.

Goldmann, G., Sweetman, A. and Warman, C. (2011). The portability of new immigrants' human capital: Language, education and occupational matching. *Queen's Economics Department Working Paper No. 1271*. Kingston, Ontario: Canada.

Gramling, D. (2009). The new cosmopolitan monolingualism: On linguistic citizenship in twenty-first century Germany. *Teaching German* 42 (2), 130–140.

Haque, E. (2012). *Multiculturalism within a bilingual framework: Language, race, and belonging in Canada*. Toronto: University of Toronto Press.

Hawthorne, L. (2008). The impact of economic selection policy on labour market outcomes for degree-qualified migrants in Canada and Australia. *IRPP Choices* 14 (5), 1–50.

Jantzen, L. (2015). Do economic principal applicants work in their intended regulated occupation?: Introducing the national household survey and immigration landing file linkage database. *Canadian Public Policy*, August, S48–S63.

Kaushal, N. and Y. Lu. (2014). Recent immigration to Canada and the United States: A mixed tale of relative selection. *International Migration Review* 49 (2), 479–522.

Knowles, M.S., et al. (1984). *Andragogy in action: Applying modern principles of adult education*. San Francisco: Jossey-Bass.

Li, P.S. (2003). Deconstructing Canada's discourse of immigrant integration. *Journal of International Migration and Integration* 4, 315–333.

Li, G. and P.K. Sah. (2019). Immigrant and refugee language policies, programs, and practices in an era of change: Promises, contradictions, and possibilities. In S. Gold and S. Nawyn (Eds.), *Routledge international handbook of migration studies* (pp. 325–338). New York: Routledge.

Lightman, N. and Good Gingrich, L. (2012). The intersecting dynamics of social exclusion: Age, gender, race and immigrant status in Canada's labour market. *Canadian Ethnic Studies*, 44 (3), 121–145.

Lippi-Green, R. (2012). *English with an accent: Language, ideology and discrimination in the United States (second edition)*. New York: Routledge.

Meinhard, A. and I. Hyman. (2012). Immigrant integration and inclusion: Investigating the Canadian partnership model from a complex-system perspective. Final Report Draft: SSHRC-Metropolis Project. Centre for Voluntary Sector Studies, Ryerson University. Toronto: Ontario.

Morgan, B. (2002). Critical practice in community-based ESL programs: A Canadian perspective. *Journal of Language, Identity, and Education* 1 (2), 141–162.

Morrow, R. and Torres, C.A. (1998). Social closure, professional domination and the new middle strata: Rethinking credentialist theories of education. In C.A. Torres & T. Mitchell (Eds.), *Sociology of education: Emerging perspectives* (pp. 121–142). Albany: State University of New York.

Ontario Human Rights Commission. 2013. Policy on removing the "Canadian Experience" barrier. Approved by the OHRC: February 1, 2013. Available at www.ohrc.on.ca

Pawlikowska-Smith, G. (2005). *Canadian language benchmarks 2000: English as a second language-for adults*. Ottawa: Citizenship and Immigration Canada.

Picot, G. and Sweetman, A. (2012). Making it in Canada: Immigration outcomes and policies. IRPP Study 29. Montréal, QC: Institute for Research on Public Policy.

Picot, G., Zhang, Y. and Hou, F. (2019). *Labour market outcomes among refugees to Canada. Analytical Studies Branch Research Paper Series 419*. Ottawa: Statistics Canada.

Reitz, J., Curtis, J. and Elrick, J. (2014). Immigrant Skill Utilization: Trends and Policy Issues. *Journal of International Migration and Integration* 15 (1), 1–26.

Ricento, T. (2013a). Measuring success when English isn't your native language: Perspectives from Canada. In P. Siemund, I. Gogolin, M.E. Schulz, and J. Davydova (Eds.), *Multilingualism and language diversity in urban areas: Acquisition, identities, space, education* (pp. 349–367). Amsterdam: John Benjamins.

Ricento, T. (2013b). The consequences of official bilingualism on the status and perception of non-official languages in Canada. *Journal of Multilingual and Multicultural Development*, 34 (5), 475–489.

Royal Commission on Bilingualism and Biculturalism. (1969). *Report of the Royal Commission on Bilingualism and Biculturalism*, Volume 4: *The Cultural Contribution of the Other Ethnic Groups*. Ottawa: Queen's Printer.

Seukwa, L.H. (2013). *Integration of refugees into the European education and labour market*. Bern: Peter Lang Publishing.

Shields, J., Drolet, J., and Valenzuela, K. (2016). Immigrant Settlement and Integration Services and the Role of Nonprofit Service Providers: A Cross-national Perspective on Trends, Issues and Evidence. *RCIS Working Paper 2016/1*. Ryerson Centre for Immigration and Settlement. Toronto: Ontario.

Shpaizman, I. (2007). The influence of neo-liberal ideas and political conflict on the privatization process of immigrant policy: A comparison of Israel, Canada and the Netherlands. Retrieved from: http://www.umd-cipe.org/conferences/Maastricht/conf_papers/Papers/The_influence_of_neo%E2%80%93liberal_ideas.pdf

Silverstein, M. (1996). Monoglot "standard" in America: Standardization and metaphors of linguistic hegemony. In D. Brenneis and R. Macaulay (Eds.), *The matrix of language: Contemporary linguistic anthropology* (pp. 284–306). Boulder, CO: Westview Press.

Statistics Canada. (2007). *Profile of language, immigration, citizenship, mobility and migration for Canada, provinces, territories and federal electoral districts (2003 Representation Order)*, 2006 Census. Ottawa: Statistics Canada.

Taylor, J. (2004). Refugees and social exclusion: What the literature says. *Migrant Action, XXVI*, 16–31.

Watt, D, Chambers, W., and MacMillan, F. (2007). Rates of language acquisition for immigrant professionals: What can we learn from English for Professional Purposes Programs? Final Report. Calgary: Faculty of Education, University of Calgary.

Wayland, S. (2006). *Unsettled: Legal and policy barriers for newcomers to Canada-Literature Review*. Canada: Community Foundation Canada.

Index[1]

A

B

C

[1] Note: Page numbers followed by 'n' refer to notes.

T. Ricento, *Refugees in Canada*,
https://doi.org/10.1007/978-3-030-76453-1

The manufacturer's authorised representative in the EU is Springer Nature Customer Service Centre GmbH, Europaplatz 3, 69115 Heidelberg, Germany. If you have any concerns regarding our products, please contact ProductSafety@springernature.com

Printed and bound by CPI Group (UK) Ltd, Croydon, CR0 4YY

30/09/2026

02225466-0011